Never Trust Any SALESPERSON

Only Trust the Facts

Jerome Berger

Copyright © 2012 by Jerome Berger. All rights reserved. Printed in the United States of America. Except as permitted under the United States Copyright Act of 1976, no part of this publication may be reproduced or distributed in any form or by any means, or stored in a database or retrieval system, without the prior written permission of the publisher.

This book has been written, distributed and sold with the intent of providing basic information in order to enlighten the reader with options when making various purchases, but does not constitute, nor is it a substitute for, legal or financial advice. The reader should consult with authoritative people specific to each subject matter. If legal, financial, or other expert advice or assistance is required, the services of a competent professional should be sought.

The listed internet addresses in this book were accurate at the time of publication. Listings and/or accuracy of the information presented within any website or film does not indicate any endorsement, in an way, whatsoever.

ISBN: 1479163597

ISBN-13: 9781479163595

About the Author

Jerome Berger is a Certified Professional Mediator and Business Intermediary with more than fifteen years of consultative and managerial experience for one of the foremost international medical supply companies, having coordinated with numerous managerial and production personnel, as well as upper management in the critical areas of Production Process, Quality Assurance, Regulatory Affairs and FDA regulations.

Additional experience working within the commercial transportation field provides an expertise of DOT rules and regulations, as they pertain to the transportation industry.

He has a vast knowledge of graphic arts, having had ownership in a full-service printing/typesetting company that served clients throughout the United States, in addition to owning and operating a commercial janitorial company.

Professional and practical activity in the field of sales, as a Manager and Front-Line Salesperson, is another avenue that qualifies him to truly understand the field of professional sales as it relates to the consumer wanting, needing, and being able to get a "fair shake" during and after the sales process. The ultimate rational objective is for all sides to receive a "fair and equitable quality result."

He has an intimate knowledge of numerous products and services such as raw and improved land, residential and commercial, business opportunities, insurance, mortgages, annuities, funeral service industry, as well as many specific product lines.

With his vast knowledge of multiple business areas ranging from management to sales, in addition to his qualifications as a Certified Professional Mediator, he now works *exclusively* helping guide all consumers as their Personal Advocate, presenting them with honest, forthright advice, mediation and negotiation services when they are confronted with crafty, deceitful, ruthless salespeople who possess no scruples.

His work as a Consumer Advocate is to provide every person with the necessary knowledge to make intelligent purchasing decisions that serve their best-interest.

His contact website is: www.AdvisingTheConsumer.org

Dedication

To my beautiful wife, Nancy,

for all her help, advice, and expertise

in the proper usage of

the written word . . .

Table of Contents

The Purpose of This Book xi

Organization of This Book xv

Chapter One 1
    Sales is an Honorable Profession

Chapter Two 5
    William Shakespeare and Sales

Chapter Three 11
    Caveat Emptor - Caveat Venditor

Chapter Four 15
    Due Diligence - aka CYA: Too Much Information - aka TMI

Chapter Five 17
    Research, Research, Research

Chapter Six 21
    The Process of the Sale: A Play in Three Acts
            (Starring the Salesperson/Actor)

Chapter Seven 35
    The Play Has Ended: Stop, Sit Back, and Relax.
    Think Critically Before Making a Decision

Chapter Eight 41
    Encore! Asking for Referrals

Chapter Nine 43
    Tips on Buying the Most Common Big Ticket Home Items:
    Think and Buy Only In Your Self-Interest

Chapter Ten 49
    Tips on Buying the Most Common Home Services:
    Think and Buy Only In Your Self-Interest

Chapter Eleven 51
    Tips on Buying or Leasing Big Ticket Items:
    Think and Buy Only In Your Self-Interest

Chapter Twelve 65
    Tips on Buying Real Estate:
    Think and Buy Only In Your Self-Interest

Chapter Thirteen 73
    Tips on Obtaining a Mortgage
    Think and Buy Only In Your Self-Interest

Chapter Fourteen 81
    Tips on Buying Intangibles:
    Think and Buy Only In Your Self-Interest

Chapter Fifteen 97
    Doublespeak: A Title by Any Other Name
        Doublespeak Titles

Chapter Sixteen 101
    More Doublespeak: When a Contract Isn't a Contract

Chapter Seventeen 103
    Open-Ended Questions

Chapter Eighteen 105
    Basic Human Emotions: Every Salesperson's Main Weapon
    Robert Plutchik's Wheel of Emotions
    Greed: The Ultimate Character Flaw

Table of Contents

Chapter Nineteen 109
    Splashy Headline Advertising: Internet - Print - Radio - TV
    Examples of Splashy Headlines

Chapter Twenty 113
    Asterisks and Disclaimers: Reading the Fine Print
    Examples of Disclaimers

Chapter Twenty-One 119
    Perception vs. Reality

Chapter Twenty-Two 123
    Time-Tested Emotional Buzzwords and Phrases
    A List of Emotional Buzzwords and Phrases

Chapter Twenty-Three 129
    Sales Seminars: In-Person and On-Line

Chapter Twenty-Four 131
    General Summation
    Important Points to Remember

Chapter Twenty-Five 133
    Helpful Websites for Consumers

Chapter Twenty-Six 137
    Hollywood Films: Where Fiction and Non-Fiction Intermingle

Chapter Twenty-Seven 139
    A Final Thought: Benefits or Consequences

Appendix A 143
    Ben Franklin Close - Critical Questions

Appendix B 145
    Ben Franklin Close - Pre-Printed Questions

The Purpose of This Book

To inform people who are willing to take the additional time required to read, and understand the unethical concepts, philosophy, and trickery that can (and is) unfortunately used in many cases, as ammunition against you, the consumer, for almost every conceivable product and service sold by unscrupulous salespeople, in order to lighten the weight in your wallet, and earn a sales commission for themselves without regard as to whether or not they are functioning in your best-interest.

Using your knowledge learned from this book, if properly applied, can help place you on a level playing field with the professional salesperson, who is taught "every trick in the book" in order to separate you from your cash. In a nutshell, that's what selling is all about to them, regardless of what any salesperson will ever tell you. They are trained to *never* express the true meaning of the sale, which is for them, their commission. Instead, they focus on your "emotional buttons" in order to ring up a sale.

Over the years there have been countless books written for salespersons to learn and/or refine the knowledge needed in the "art of selling." While many have genuinely proceeded to teach and develop the skills necessary to become an ethical, professional salesperson, they can also teach the reader the fine art of word manipulation that can (and in many sales pitches) is used to snooker you, the consumer to purchase products and services negative to your self-interest. These instructional books have been primarily written for the benefit of the salesperson, not you the consumer. What is never discussed is that word and body language manipulation can and should be a two-way street. Therefore, there is no reason for any consumer "doing battle" with the salesperson not to have the advantage of being on as level a playing field as possible. After all, it's your money. Protect it.

This book was written with the intent of enlightening, and therefore benefiting the consumer, by getting right to the point, "telling it like it is." Every person spending their money is entitled to receive truthful information about the sales process, in order to have a "fighting chance" in the art of "mental fisticuffs" that takes place almost every time you are looking to purchase a product or service. You are entitled to have a positive experience during, and after, the completion of the sale. The knowledge in this book can help you achieve that experience.

Most any person who has purchased a product or service has witnessed, or has been involved, in a full Broadway production of the "sales play" that has been running all over the world, in countless languages, for thousands of years. The game of sales has been, and always will be, the same. To paraphrase William Shakespeare, 'only the players change.'

One of the most powerful tactics salespeople use in their arsenal is the strategy of creating urgency. Phrases such as "This is the end of the run," "There won't be any more available for at least a year," "This one is the last of its kind," all create a sense of urgency. These statements may or may not be true. If they are, you must decide if the purchase is still in your best-interest. If your emotions can be reached, because you are led to *believe* the deal of the century is about to pass you by, and you cannot live without whatever is being sold, the salespersons hook will reel you in like a fish in the ocean.

It's very important to always remember: You have lived without whatever the salesperson is selling, and can certainly continue to do so a while longer, while you think about it critically. The product or

The Purpose of This Book

service you are intending to buy will probably be there tomorrow, either from the salesperson you are dealing with, or from another salesperson from a competing company. If not, a substitute can take its place, or perhaps you may come to realize you never really needed to buy what you thought you "had to have." The world is not going to come to an end because you didn't make that "one big purchase," even though the advertising industry wants you to think otherwise. In most cases, the sense of urgency is your mortal enemy. Fight that emotion and you will generally be better off for it.

If you have already concluded, prior to speaking with any salesperson, that you are truly in need of what you are seeking, then you must be ready for the ensuing *war* to come, which is the sales process.

The basis of all sales is to buy low and sell high. The difference is a "fair profit" the company earns, minus all expenses, which includes the sales commission. When any salesperson is employed, a "fair commission" is also earned by them for time spent selling the product or service being offered.

Thus, the key word *fair* becomes a critical factor regarding this process. Fair is a relative term. Depending on which party in the transaction you ask, the answer to some is: *"Fair is in the mind of the beholder."* Imbedded within the DNA of human beings are the imperfections of greed and selfishness, neither of which correlate to *fair*, thereby placing the sales profession into an automatic adversarial relationship between buyer and seller.

You most probably will see on any salespersons desk or business card presented to you, a title other than *salesperson*. The reason for this substitution is to divert your attention from the thought of having to confront a salesperson (a title disliked by most people), lulling you into *feeling* more at ease with a more likeable term such as *representative*. Always remember, regardless of title, you are speaking with a salesperson seeking to earn a commission as a result of your purchasing a product or service. A list of many varied replacement titles can be found in chapter fifteen.

Never Trust Any Salesperson

Selling has been a deceptive profession since the first interaction took place between two people, trying to outwit each other. The primary purpose in today's marketplace is to lure an individual into the purchase of a product or service that will earn a commission, and possibly a bonus. As a consumer, always be on guard for the *unscrupulous, manipulative* salesperson sometimes working you with their *charm,* and in other instances, placing pressure on your emotions, to lead you into a purchase you may very well regret, perhaps for a lifetime. If applied diligently, the information within, may help provide you, the consumer, the opportunity to "level the playing field," which is the primary purpose of this book. Think me myself and I, always maintaining your self-interest when speaking with any salesperson. Your future purchases depend on it.

"A writer's job is to tell the truth."

Andy Rooney
Writer, Philosopher, Curmudgeon, Thinker
(January 14, 1919 - November 4, 2011)

Organization of This Book

This book has been organized into separate chapters dealing with many different aspects of the sales process. Some discuss the negative implications that can happen if you are not overly cautious. Other chapters are more philosophical, but are just as critical in order to understand why, and how, people function with each other the way they do, in order to gain the maximum results each side is seeking to achieve. Chapters Nine through Fourteen contain *tips* on what to think about before buying some of life's most important products and services. They contain many general, but important, questions to ask any salesperson. In addition there are two "Ben Franklin Close" pages, Appendix A being blank for you to fill in important questions specific to a purchase, and Appendix B, pre-written with general questions already included. Copy and enlarge these specific pages for any present or future important purchases you are considering.

Feel free to skip around and read the chapters you want to immediately know about. This book has been written for informational purposes only, and doesn't have to be read as a novel.

In order to be fully armed and ready for the ensuing battle, having the knowledge needed to protect yourself against the ruthlessness of the many salespersons in the marketplace, it will behoove you to take the time and devour every chapter be it practical and/or philosophical, in order to understand the true concept of sales as it relates to human nature. Each chapter serves its own purpose toward understanding the numerous aspects you will be confronted with when seeking to make a purchase. You bought this book to learn how to protect your money by purchasing wisely from this moment on, with your self-interest in mind. Nothing less will do. You, the reader, have a right to be just as ruthless protecting your assets, as those who would benefit by increasing theirs, at your expense.

Knowing the information prior to meeting any salesperson, legitimate or not, will arm you with the knowledge needed so you don't get financially "taken to the cleaners." An improper purchase can sometimes have devastating consequences, especially in areas such as purchasing a home, or a specific financial product. This is very serious business. If you don't purchase what functions in your self-interest, it doesn't affect the salesperson. The commission has been made, and it's on to the next prospect, also known as a lead. Should you end up being dissatisfied, you would never refer the salesperson to anyone you know. However, from a realistic standpoint, only a small percentage of salespeople are professionals who actually seek and work referrals (read chapter eight.) They are generally always looking for new leads. An example would be within an arena where people are required to come to them (such as a car dealership). They can spend a vast portion of any day watching and waiting for their next mark.

Purchasing a product or service is a process. "Clear thinking" of the mind translates to a "warm and fuzzy" feeling in the heart. Know all aspects of what you are buying, prior to signing on the dotted line. Otherwise, you may find yourself with a disastrous case of "buyer's remorse," asking yourself whether or not you made the right decision.

We all need to purchase products and services throughout our lives. It's a fact-of-life. There is nothing wrong with this, as long as we pursue and purchase with our rational self-interest in mind at all times, leaving our emotions at the door.

Chapter One

Sales is an Honorable Profession

As defined by a dictionary: *Sales is the transfer of title to property from one party to another for a price.* In human terms, sales can also be defined as an art: *The art of persuasion.* The underlining human moral concerns of "fair and equitable" have consistently been an issue salespeople have tackled and struggled with since the dawn of time. This subject will undoubtedly continue to remain a human issue *indefinitely.*

There is absolutely nothing inherently wrong with any person seeking to earn a living in the sales profession. It's an honest way for any person wanting to provide for themselves and their family, an authentic livelihood, as long as your needs and requirements as a consumer are met in a conscientious, fair, equitable, forthright manner.

Salespeople instinctively know that treating and placing their clients/customers first, will in the long-run bring financial rewards to them through increased production, referrals, bonuses, etc. It is imperative you know if they have or have not chosen to function within the framework of that philosophy. Think about it for a moment. They too are consumers, however, human nature dictates. It depends on which *hat* the salesperson is wearing during any given time.

Due to the structure of most sales positions that have been designed to operate on a commission basis, utilizing draws against commission, (if a draw even exists) human nature invariably rules. Many succumb to the intense pressure to perform at any cost. This pressure comes from management personnel up the food chain, looking out for their piece of the pie, which is the override. If a sale is not made, the salesperson on commission doesn't eat, nor does the mortgage get paid, and the sales manager doesn't receive their percentage, thereby placing additional pressure on everyone involved working in commissioned sales.

One important element of economics depends on "something being sold to someone." People have been purchasing products and services for thousands of years, and will assuredly continue to do so. Hopefully, the salesperson and you, the consumer, will thrive upon completion of the selling process. It should be designed to be a "win-win" situation, but unfortunately in a non-perfect world it does not always work that way. Historically, the subject of ethics has never been in the forefront for most salespeople, and is non-existent for some. The primary objective has generally been and will continue to be, about "making the sale" at any cost, period. No further discussion required. Most salespeople under a truth serum would readily admit so.

The primary purpose of the widely accepted commission incentive is designed to reward and motivate sales people to sell more and more. Most companies are structured to pay their sales force in the range of 1% - 10% of the sale, though exceptions exist within higher ranges as well. It's very important to understand the commission paid to the salesperson is really being paid by you, the consumer, for if the sales force were eliminated, the market could allow the company to pass along the savings. Hence, the reason why some companies will spend a portion of their marketing capital on direct-to-consumer sales through advertising and mailings. It can be less expensive, and they can reach a wider target market, choosing to pass along the savings by means of reduced prices that will allow the company to be more competitive and possibly more profitable.

It's critical to note even if a salesperson is not involved, the direct sale of a product or service and the terms (if any), must be completely understood in order to serve your self-interest. Working with an *ethical* salesperson looking out for your best-interest could prove to be less expensive and have greater value in the long run, even though you still paid a commission.

This book was not written to castigate or demean salespeople, or the profession. Its purpose is to provide enlightenment and knowledge to you, the consumer, and expose the seedy side of the sales process you must always be cognizant of anytime you purchase a product or service. In a perfect world this issue would not exist. However, the instinct of self-interest can, and does, overtake ethics within the mind of many salespeople in order to earn a commission at any cost. This can obviously mean you, the consumer, may end up on the losing side of the sale.

A Final Thought
Always seek out the answer for this one consistent question *any* time you are speaking with *any* salesperson. **Is this salesperson working for or against my/our self-interest, or do they only care about "closing the sale" and receiving a commission at any cost?**

"Selling is an art. Purchasing is, as well."

Chapter Two

William Shakespeare and Sales

You may ask what in the world does Shakespeare have to do with sales. The answer is: A lot. It's all summed up in the lines of two of his plays: *As You Like It,* and *Hamlet.*

As You Like It - "All the world's a stage, and all the men and women are merely players"

Hamlet - "The play's the thing"

Regardless of how one chooses to look at it, these two very famous quotes are a fact of life in our everyday interactions with people. The concept of what all people must do to provide a decent standard of living for themselves, and others, can have a different meaning to each individual. Even those not working in sales, who never, think of themselves as salespersons, *sell* on a day-to-day basis in the workplace.

The product they are selling is; *themselves.* Many people function as actors on a stage within their daily lives, when they speak to someone they may not necessarily like, or care to be with. However, they have no choice but to interact with them and *get along* in order to earn a livelihood.

Most people have "friends at work" and "true friends." The day you stop working at any one company, is most probably the day you will cease to ever see your "friends at work." You may have literally hundreds of "friends at work," but can generally count on one hand the number of "true friends" you have. Thinking rationally about it, you realize your "friends at work" are generally just acquaintances. It is what it is. Reality can be a stark and awesome thing.

Your relationship with any salesperson is no different. This book is about the reality of interaction between two or more human beings who are just acquaintances, interacting for a business purpose. One person is a buyer, and another a salesperson(s). The entire process is a *performance,* by the salesperson(s), no matter how the sales industry massages/spins, what the profession refers to as a *presentation.*

An extremely important rule to always adhere to is: Never think of any salesperson as your *friend*, regardless of your relationship. Be it family, personal friend, or acquaintance, the interaction between consumer and salesperson must be played-out in a business-like manner. As outlined in chapter six, it's a theatrical play. Business and pleasure rarely mix well, within the context of purchasing from a salesperson, and when they do, it could be classified as a theatrical farce.

"Neither a borrower nor a lender be" is a famous line in Shakespeare's play, *Hamlet*. In addition, an old Scottish proverb states: "Lend your money and lose your friend." A modern version takes this one step further, as to why the distinction between money and friends should remain separate: "I had some money and a friend. I lent my money to my friend. I lost my money and my friend."

Think of your day at *work* as being a *play*, because your *real personality* comes out when you walk out the door. The very same concept can be applied to the sales process. The salesperson is an actor who, through learned instruction, has honed the craft of acting. It's no different than going to the theatre to watch a play, where the objective is to subdue the audience into believing the performance taking place is real, the difference being you are the character in the play seeking to purchase with your hard-earned money. It's time to" level the playing field," for you the consumer, as you are just as capable of winning an Academy Award, depending on how well you play your role. The salesperson functions in their capacity every day, playing various roles depending on the personality and intelligence of the person(s) they are working with. They know the "tricks of the trade" that can separate you from the money in your wallet. It's your responsibility to be certain you are receiving the very best return from whatever was purchased.

Purchasing a product or service from any salesperson creates, by its very nature an adversarial relationship. The salesperson wants the sale to culminate at the highest cost and (possibly along with that) the lowest benefits possible, unless they are paid-for *add-ons*. You want the exact opposite. Both parties in any sales transaction are always functioning in their own self-interest.

In the world of sales the "warm-up" is one of the oldest tricks in the book designed to disarm you, the buyer, by lulling you into a subtle form of hypnosis, controlling every phase of the sales process. It's like leading sheep to the slaughter. However crass that may sound, it is reality, make no mistake about it. You cannot hope to win the *war* if you are not properly prepared for the *battle*.

Three Important Rules to Remember During the "Sales Performance"
Rule No. 1 - Intimidation. Always remember when speaking to a salesperson, whether for the first time or within an on-going business

relationship such as a "Stock Broker," "Financial Planner," or whatever other title is stated on their business card: *Never* under any circumstances, allow yourself to feel or become intimidated. Should you decide to serve your interests better, by severing your relationship, because you have found another salesperson you think will better meet your specific needs, expect resistance, as the result of your decision, will incur a loss of future commissions for them.

Listen carefully to any salesperson for the reasons as to why you should maintain a business relationship with them. After thoughtful consideration, make a rational decision serving only your self-interest. The salesperson/actor is your acquaintance, even though you may have utilized their services in the past. It may be time to move on if your self-interest is not being met presently. This includes your best friend and/or your favorite relative. This is just another reason why it's better *not to mix business with pleasure*. Obviously, there are exceptions. Pick and choose them with care.

Rule No. 2 - Never *like, love,* or *care about,* any product or service until you fully complete your purchase, knowing you have made the very best deal possible, having served your self-interest. There will be plenty of time to enjoy the emotional/financial value of your product or service, knowing you have accomplished your primary business objectives first and foremost.

Rule No. 3 - Don't ever fall for the *charisma* a salesperson may portray, such as the *phony smile* or *friend routine,* as there are no friends when it comes to money. Their phony routine of functioning within a dual role of salesperson and actor may be one and the same, with variations they think will benefit their bottom line. They will begin with small talk. If a child is with you, be assured a compliment will be forthcoming, telling you how cute they are. *Its show-time folks!* This is a common warm-up sales tactic that is designed to lower your guard. You must always be aware your relationship with any salesperson is adversarial by its very nature. You both want the same result: *A sale.* However, the issue is *how to get there.* Your business relationship with the salesperson/actor is "all about the money," regardless of what *script* or *role* is played by the salesperson/actor during the *play*.

"A friend to all is a friend to none."

Aristotle
Greek Philosopher
(384 B.C.-322 B.C.)

Chapter Three

Caveat Emptor
Caveat Venditor

Caveat Emptor - Latin for "Let the Buyer Beware." This well-known phrase has probably been around as long as salespeople have been selling their goods and services. This very wise anonymous quote rings as true in today's marketplace as the day it was conceived, and for the very same reasons. Someone, somewhere in the annals of time was "taken to the cleaners," "sold a bill of goods," or "paid too much." Whatever the issue, the buyer was not pleased with the purchase. It is all the more reason why it's important to understand that "knowledge is power." Use it for your objective(s) and benefit(s) during the sales process.

Caveat Venditor - Latin for "Let the Seller Beware." This little known phrase places the burden on the seller to take responsibility for the product or service being sold. Self-protection from lawsuits is the major reason why Errors and Omissions insurance is generally required for many people working in the financial and real estate industry. Keep this in mind at all times, especially when purchasing anything of consequence.

Everyone is a Salesperson

Every person you buy a product or service from, be it the "butcher" in the grocery store, the "service advisor" you first meet at any automobile repair facility, or the "interior decorator" you just hired to spruce up your home, is a salesperson behind the scene. For them, it's all about transferring as much money from your wallet to theirs, via the art of selling. Many salespeople you regularly deal with receive an additional commission if they can "up-sell" you, even though you may not realize what is actually happening. Most businesses prefer to operate that way with their salespeople in order to increase profits, by placing an incentive on the salesperson to suggest alternatives and/or add-ons that can turn into a more profitable sale. At times, a suggestion from the person you are speaking with may seem to be just that, however, in reality the purpose of the supposed suggestion is only about selling. It's certainly possible that whatever was suggested by the salesperson may be the right way to go, but maybe not. It's always up to you, the buyer to think critically while you contemplate the decision to buy or not to buy.

"In this world nothing can be said to be certain, except death and taxes."

Benjamin Franklin
Polymath and one of the founding fathers of the United States
(January 17, 1706 - April 17, 1790)

As the above quote pertains to sales, the word *disappointment* can be added to the lives of people who choose not to be Socratic critical thinkers regarding the vast number of purchases made during one's lifetime. A reasoned evaluation of your future purchases will benefit you enormously. Beware *any* advertisement *or* salesperson stating the product or service is *free*. It's one of the foremost mirages used to entice or close a sale. No company is in business to lose money by "giving away something for free," therefore, no salesperson is ever going to offer anything for *free* without the expressed authority of the company. Anytime you are being offered something for *free,* the profit margins have been buried elsewhere. However, as a consumer, you will probably never know where, or how much.

"There's no such thing as a free lunch."

Anonymous

Chapter Four

Due Diligence - aka CYA
Too Much Information - aka TMI

Due Diligence
Due Diligence is a well-known term spoken in polite society, as a substitution for the slang term better known as CYA, one of the most important phrases in any language. Some consider it vulgar, due to its direct meaning of "cover your ass." Regardless of how you, the reader choose to speak, it all boils down to the same thing.

Due Diligence/CYA is imperative when considering the purchase of anything more than a pack of chewing gum. Without proceeding into the process of knowing whether a purchase is, or is not, beneficial for you, was bought at the best price and terms possible before signing any contract, can lead to very detrimental consequences.

With this in mind, the reader of this book, in addition to being a consumer, must circumvent the unscrupulous salesperson only buying from those who are willing to sell their wares ethically with your best-interest always in their mind, *even if the commission is less*. Unfortunately, it is not always easy to find such an individual, however, *they are out there*. This is only one aspect of due diligence that can and must be accomplished in order to achieve your goals. Please note, the term "your goals," and not the goals of the salesperson, for after the sale both parties go their own way. It must be remembered even if you see each other sometime after the sale, you are the one left *living* with whatever was purchased. The primary objective of the salesperson, which is to sell, has been accomplished and the commission has been collected. You should rightfully receive the direct benefit from the sale if you purchased wisely.

Too Much Information

One element often taking place within the sales process as you are speaking with a salesperson, that is *not in your best-interest* is the release of "too much information," whether it is verbal or through readable body language.

Be cautious about letting the salesperson know what you are thinking. You're first responsibility is to collect as much information as possible, which may require you to interview multiple salespeople. Only give the salesperson information you know will provide, what you need to make a rational decision that is in your self- interest.

Giving out too much information can easily be portrayed through your body language, without realizing the buying signals you are giving out. Any professional salesperson selling a product or service, will always be looking for any type of signals you may inadvertently be sending. Should they sense an emotionally positive response toward your desiring to own what they are trying to sell, they will use the opening, and expand their sales techniques in such a way, you may never be aware of what is actually taking place.

Chapter Five

Research, Research, Research

One of the most important elements of the sale takes place long before you ever meet the salesperson. It's your responsibility, and in your self-interest, to spend whatever time it takes to research your future purchases, especially if the product or service can have either a beneficial or detrimental effect on you and/or those persons you care about.

The power of the internet makes it easier than ever to research any product or service in order to obtain comprehensive knowledge of what you are looking for. In order to be successful, it's imperative to thoroughly perform your *due diligence*. It's the master key required in order to derive the correct information to make a rational, intelligent decision serving your self-interest.

After obtaining your basic research, save a lot of shoe leather, make life easy on yourself, then start to narrow down the salespeople you wish to interview through the use of your phone. Your requirements may very well be important enough for you to personally interview the salesperson you truly think will meet your specific needs and wants. Please note the use of the word *interview*. Always think of your interaction as an interview, as it will help you maintain control throughout the process. Utilizing your acting abilities (two can play the game), let each prospective salesperson know exactly what your criteria is for the service or product you are speaking about.

A very important part of your acting ability is to convince the salesperson you are intelligent and mean business. In no uncertain (but always polite terms), let them know what you want, when you want it, and inform them you will continue your search until you find the salesperson who can deliver your requirements. Your personal persona is the best weapon you have to generate a presentation to the salesperson that you are not going to necessarily be an easy sale. However, if you are speaking with a true professional, that salesperson will have received enough information from you to know the finalization of any sale will be more than worthwhile to them. The professional/ethical salesperson, knowing their market, will almost always be patient and willing to work in your best-interest, while an amateur/con artist will disappear from the scene.

Review chapter twenty-five for listed websites that can enhance your basic research for your intended purpose. As important as it is to know *what you know,* it is just as critical to be aware of *what you don't know.* No one person knows everything. Comprehensive research is the key.

The following products and services are prime examples regarding the importance of performing documented research prior to meeting any salesperson. As you become more knowledgeable about the product or service you should take your new-found information and kick your research up another level. There is no limit as to how many times this process should be repeated. Your research will be finished when it's finished, and you are thoroughly satisfied with the results of knowing precisely what you are looking for and who will meet your needs.

The list below is a sampling of important representations for important items many people purchase throughout their lifetime. Chapters Nine through Fourteen present a methodical method regarding the process for proper research. They can provide a format for thinking methodically about what you are seeking to purchase. Let any salesperson know they are speaking to an intelligent prospect. If they have any brains at all, they will act accordingly. Otherwise, move on. "Seek and Ye shall find!"

Home Items	Home Services	Big Ticket Items	Real Estate	Intangibles
Flooring	Carpenters	Cars	Residential	Annuities
Furniture	Electricians	Boats	Commercial Mortgage	Life Insurance
Heating/ Cooling Systems	Plumbers			Funerals - The Final Purchase
			Reverse Mortgage	
Home Siding and Roofing				
Major Appliances				

"Basic research is what I am doing when I don't know what I am doing."

Werner Von Braun
Preeminent rocket engineer and chief architect for the Saturn V launch vehicle for the Apollo spacecraft.
(March 23, 1912 - June 16, 1977)

Chapter Six

The Process of the Sale: A Play in Three Acts (Starring the Salesperson/Actor)

Act I

The Introduction and Warm-up

You make an appointment to meet and interview with the salesperson/actor after any number of conversations. Please note the word *interview*. You're the boss. It's your money and they are the one who wants it. *Always* be the person sitting in the driver's seat. If you ever allow any salesperson/actor to control you, instead of you controlling them, you may find yourself being quite upset with what you have purchased and/or been driven off a financial cliff.

Depending on the personality, intellect, and character of the salesperson/actor, the "well-rehearsed presentation/pitch" of Act I will begin pleasantly enough by introducing themselves with generally accepted formalities. They are working toward building a rapport, which translates into trust, then a sale.

As the play is unfolding, the salesperson/actor is warming up and researching you by your appearance, demeanor, articulation, etc. You can perform the same research on them, from your vantage point. You're being "sized up" as to whether you utilize logic or emotion in your decision making. It's a guide as to which avenue of attack will be articulated in order to make a sale. To quote Albert Einstein, "A little knowledge is a dangerous thing. So is a lot." Use the knowledge you achieved during your research, for your benefit only.

Don't Feel Shy or Intimidated

It's very important you earn, and win, the Academy Award for best actor, never letting the salesperson/actor know what you are actually thinking, for they are doing the very same thing. Both you, and the salesperson/actor, are collecting information on each other. If your intellect and guts tells you as the play continues; the person you are dealing with is not suitable to meet your needs, request another salesperson. You are the one spending your hard earned money, and the salesperson/actor is the one who wants it.

Always, be aware one of the most serious sins any salesperson/actor can commit is answering their cell phone or checking their text messages. It's unprofessional and rude. This is the time you should have their undivided attention. If it should happen to you during a one-on-one sales presentation/pitch, and the salesperson/actor doesn't even bother to ask your permission, unless the call or message pertains to you, it's time to leave or ask for another salesperson/actor. If they're upset: That's their problem. They are probably not working for or concerned about your best-interest. You owe them nothing except common courtesy. In return, they owe you professionalism when speaking about the product or service they are selling, and common courtesy.

The act will proceed for as long as the salesperson/actor thinks is required, in order to disarm your instinctive and learned innermost feelings about salespeople/actors. One of the oldest tricks utilized when speaking with a salesperson/actor, be it in your home or an office, is for the salesperson/actor to glance around at your surroundings for any clues as to your likes, dislikes, political affiliations, family photos, hobbies, etc. They may very well choose one or more subjects viewed they feel comfortable talking about during this process. If the meeting is at their place of business, they only have the ammunition of honing in on basic personal information they have stored, such as your general appearance, manner, and speech in order to surmise the best way to *work* you. This entire process can take anywhere from five to thirty minutes. This initial connection works, or it doesn't.

Act II

Getting Down to Business

Once the niceties have run their course, the real reason for the meeting takes place. This is definitely the time to pull up your antennas, put on your body armor, and proceed with caution.

Q and A Time - This is a very good thing for both you, and the salesperson/actor to do. If the salesperson/actor does not take the time to probe and ask meaningful questions, they are not doing their job. Essentially, this is a "red flag" as they are merely acting as an order taker. They may not possess the service or product knowledge needed for what they are selling, or they may just be a "run-of-the-mill" amateur, not willing or caring to take the proper amount of time necessary to learn your needs. They are only interested in a sale, without trying to find out your requirements. A well-qualified, ethical salesperson/actor will take all the time necessary and listen, in order to provide the answer(s) for the service or product best suited for you, regardless of commission.

The Sales Presentation/Pitch - Depending on the intelligence, product knowledge, and class of the salesperson/actor making the delivery, you will have to make a determination as to whether or not you wish to continue the play or move on. Regardless of which decision you make, remember, all salespeople/actors have the same objective: To make a sale. Pay attention to the body language and mannerisms portrayed by the salesperson/actor. It's critical you get past their charade, as quickly as possible in order to determine if the salesperson/actor you are speaking with is working with your best-interest in mind.

The Objection Phase - Salespeople/actors are always ready for objections. Objections are Sales 101 in any sales manual or sales training session. It's all about manipulating you with clever terminology until your protective barriers are torn down and you're ready to surrender by signing on the dotted line.

One of the most overused strategies in any sales meeting has always been, "the sale begins when the customer says no." Perhaps this may be the case, perhaps not. It's always up to you. There is certainly nothing wrong with an objection being raised on your part. You owe it to yourself, and it's expected by any salesperson/actor. Another way of looking at an objection is to see it as an unanswered question. If the salesperson/actor knows their *stuff*, they will answer appropriately, and the answer may just be the information you need to make a decision to purchase or not. Should you read them as getting a bit testy or demonstrating body language that says they can't wait to get on to the next prospect, i.e., floating eye contact for other fish to fry if you are in a showroom situation, or checking their watch, then it's time to take your business elsewhere.

More Q and A - At this point you may have additional questions. Proceed through this phase until you are fully satisfied with all the answers. If you are not, then additional research could be in order, or perhaps you need to speak to another salesperson and/or company.

Cost-Benefit-Value Analysis

Calculations, properly executed, will provide you with the answer(s) required, to justify your purchase. There are many avenues to consider financially as well as lifestyle. Don't necessarily depend on any salesperson/actor to develop a Cost-Benefit-Value Analysis scenario for you. It takes time and thought. However, if the salesperson is a true professional they will help you develop this analysis in order to consummate a quality sale. That's a "win-win" scenario!

Questions to consider for Cost-Benefit-Value Analysis

- Is your purchase a viable financial strategy, as compared to the perceived benefit you wish to receive?
- Does the value exceed the cost?
- Does the purchase fit into your age and lifestyle?
- Is the cost justified when calculating the benefit and value of the purchase?
- Is the cost viable when compared to the present market?
- Are the payments/overhead affordable based on income, responsibilities, net worth, etc.?

Negotiation

The most critical phase of this act is about to be played out. This is where the "rubber meets the road." You have spent valuable time looking for a service or product that meets your needs, and you think you may have found it. The answer will depend on your negotiating skills that will evaluate the outcome you seek to achieve. Ask yourself if all three of the most basic elements about your prospective purchase are being met using the Cost-Benefit-Value Analysis procedures. The higher the stakes regarding the purchase, the greater consideration each individual element must receive.

The art of the negotiation process has been written about for centuries. In a perfect world, the negotiation process and outcome will always benefit both parties equally, universally known as "win-win." However, due to imperfections imbedded in the DNA of people this is not always the case. One of the most primal, powerful forces of nature almost always kicks in, the concept of self-interest to the detriment of the opposing party. Morality can, and does, take a back seat in the mind of many a salesperson/actor when it comes down to making or not making a sale. The ultimate objective of being able to provide for themselves and/or their family is cause number one. Therefore, you the consumer must always function in your self-interest as well, with no regrets. After all, negotiating is a form of war. The only difference is the weapon of choice, a pen instead of a gun. However, make no mistake the outcome can be quite deadly from a financial standpoint, if you don't negotiate properly.

Ten Important Rules to Always Remember when Negotiating in Your Self-Interest

Rule No. 1 - Know your adversary. The salesperson/actor may very well be a true "professional" meaning they work their livelihood seriously and can be quite skilled at word manipulation (read chapters fifteen and sixteen), though they will never admit to it. They are well trained by their managers, read proprietary marketing material and role-play, always continuing to perfect the *art of persuasion*.

Negotiation skills are academically thought of as being able to convince your adversary to see your point of view, pertaining to the give-and-take discussion taking place, with both sides coming out on top. However, many salespersons/actors choose to inherently not view negotiation this way. To them it's about winning first, compromise second, as the compromise may mean less commission, or possibly no commission due to the loss of a sale. For the average consumer, it's like going into battle bare without armor, while the enemy is armed to the teeth. Certainly, quite a task, but definitely achievable if you apply the rules needed to win the war.

Rule No. 2 - Do your homework through good research. Research is your best friend. The knowledge you will have accumulated is what the salesperson/actor does not want you to know. It can make their job more difficult, with the outcome possibly being no sale for them, as you may decide not to buy, or take your business elsewhere. You must demonstrate you are not the average consumer, and will purchase only when it serves your self-interest, not theirs. Don't hesitate to bring any research information with you. Any salesperson/actor confronted with your research notes will most probably respect and speak to you on a higher level than the average prospect.

Rule No. 3 - Ask multiple questions. Use the rule of the five W's and one H: Who? What? Where? When? Why? How? "Why not?" and "What if?" should also be added as possible alternative ammunition in order to obtain all the information that is available for you to receive exactly what you want. Taking enough time to properly pursue your needs and interests may very well give you just about as much knowledge of the service or product that the salesperson/actor has acquired.

Rule No 4 - Never become emotional over the product or service. Fall in love with it after the sale, when you own it. This is one of the prime weapons in the arsenal of any salesperson/actor. Don't ever allow the salesperson/actor to neutralize the logical part of your thinking process, through psychological manipulation. IF you buy right, you will have plenty of time to truly enjoy your purchase, after the sale.

If the negotiations are not streaming toward your self-interest, or you are being pressured, you can always pull out the heavy artillery by telling the salesperson/actor politely but firmly a statement such as: "Up to this point in time, I have never owned this item before and, without meeting my needs, I can continue to live very nicely without it." You have just moved the bar, letting the salesperson/actor know you mean business. It's important to remember, the salesperson/actor may very well want the sale more than you do. Maintain your options, such as getting the very same service or product elsewhere.

Rule No. 5 - Never, under any circumstances, accept the first offer presented. Regardless of the product or service: Tangible or intangible. You and the salesperson/actor have just left the starting gate and the race is far from over. Knowing how to negotiate is your key to getting what you want, including the best applicable terms.

Rule No. 6 - Always seek alternatives that meet your requirements. Unless it's unrealistic, do not change your requirements. You need what you need, and you're the one spending the money to make the purchase. If an alternative is legitimately viable than you have negotiated well, and should be quite satisfied after the sale. A different color that will please you, shorter or longer length of terms, a different delivery time, or a financial product that is more conducive to your personal lifestyle. The list can be limitless. Know exactly what you are looking for and stick with it. Negotiating can sometimes mean making concessions. If your concessions are truly acceptable to your ultimate objectives, you are functioning in your self-interest. Making concessions can be a two-way street. The salesperson/actor or sales manager/actor has, in many cases, the power to make concessions on their part in order to get your business. "Ask, and you shall receive!"

Rule No. 7 - They want to sell it more than you want to buy it. Keep yourself in the driver's seat at all times. For example: The end of the month, quarter or year may be closing in. The product or service has to move in time for new models, benefits, etc. This reality of bottom-line pressure in sales is universal. The greater your knowledge about the service or product, the higher probability your purchase will serve your self-interest.

Rule No. 8 - Take your time. The well-worn expression "time is of the essence" has no place when it comes to negotiating. The exact opposite is your weapon of choice. Never allow yourself to get intimidated by the process. Your purchase may take more than one meeting, and numerous phone calls and/or emails. If that's what it takes in order for you to achieve your objective, than you must do what you must do in order for your goals to be met. In any negotiation, patience is an absolute requirement if success is to be achieved.

Rule No. 9 - Never assume anything. It's very dangerous and can get you into a lot of hot water. You must "know," regarding the subject at hand: Whether it's price, color, style, options, terms, interest rate, conditions, stability of product, service or company. Know what you are looking for, write it down, and live by it. You want what you want, and are entitled to receive exactly what will fulfill your needs, as long as it's realistic. Don't settle for less.

Rule No. 10 - Pull out your trump card and tell the salesperson/actor to "beat" the competition. The salesperson/actor knows, and you should not hesitate to remind them, they are not the only game in town. Note the word "meet" was not mentioned (as you may see in advertising). Why ask them to "meet" the competition, when you might as well tell them to "beat" them. This may be in price, terms or both.

If you have given a winning performance, and accomplished what you wanted at the price, terms, and applicable conditions, you deserve congratulatory kudos. You have just won the Oscar in the Best Actor category. Even though the salespersons/actors commission will be smaller, it certainly is better for them as well, instead of getting a big, fat, goose egg for all the time and effort spent with you, had you made a decision to take-a-walk. It's very important to understand the flexibility many salespeople/actors know they have, regarding price and/or terms, etc., of the product or service for sale. They almost always know their flexibility pertaining to the bottom-line price point, prior to actually needing their managers OK. It's not necessarily in their financial interest to let you know. They would rather charm you into a high price which will compensate into a higher commission. It's one of the "dirty little secrets" in sales.

If all else fails, and you cannot come to an agreement, it's time to take a walk. You may be pleasantly surprised to be told there just may be *something* they can do. If you give the salesperson/actor your phone number or email, don't be surprised if you are contacted with a better offer. It happens all the time.

Act III

The Close - The game of "mental fisticuffs" has culminated to the point the salesperson/actor will hone in like a shark for the kill, in order to close the sale thereby justifying the time spent with you. Without the close, the sales process is incomplete for the salesperson/actor.

Should you make a decision not to buy (for any number of reasons), during this phase of the *play*, you have to do what you have to do, always in your self-interest. Never feel pressured into allowing the close to take place, even if you don't know where the same service or product, of the same or higher quality, can be delivered less expensively. Take away with you any information you received, which may invariably help you research other vendors.

Be on guard when it comes time for the close, (which can happen anytime) as that is the ultimate goal of the salesperson/actor, and is always in play whether you realize it or not. The salesperson/actor is *always* looking for the verbal and nonverbal clues that can give them an indication it's time to try to close the sale. The following list provides some of the most common closing techniques. Be aware of them.

Should you wish to investigate one of the most basic, "real world" entertaining segments pertaining to the "bottom line" purpose any salesperson works toward, which is to *close the sale,* view the ABC (Always Be Closing*)* scene at the beginning of the acclaimed film: Glengarry Glen Ross. There is more "truth than poetry" to that scene. Viewing the entire film will provide you with insight into the "world of sales" as it truly is, regardless, how it is dressed up to appear.

Be in charge. Only allow the salesperson/actor to close the sale because you are totally satisfied all your requirements have been met during and after the play, including all applicable terms and conditions. Should you really want to be proactive, tell the salesperson/actor upfront you do not want them to try to close you. Instead, you will tell them when you are ready to close. This upside down technique is generally very unusual for a salesperson/actor to hear, but it works. It relieves you from some of the "game playing," and lets the salesperson/actor know you are not the average mark. Utilize all your acting abilities in order to convince the salesperson/actor you are a serious, intelligent person, who insists on being treated as such.

The following *closes* are a sampling of what you may hear from a salesperson/actor during Act III.

The Affordable Close

- I can get this to fit comfortably in your price range.
- The cost per unit is the lowest in the marketplace.
- If you figure this over time, it proves to be very reasonable.
- This will only cost you $1.50 a day to own.

The Choices Close

- No question about it. One of these three will work for you.

The Compliment Close

- This really makes you look younger.
- You look like a million dollars behind the wheel.

The Demo Close

- A pre-planned demonstration guaranteed to excite the emotions.

The Sense of Urgency Close

- The inventory is very limited at the warehouse.
- The raw material is increasing in price. The time to buy is now.
- This is a "Once-in-a-lifetime" opportunity.
- This is a one day sale only.

The Take-Away Close

- Our special runs through today only. I can throw in two for the price of one if you buy now.

The Trial Close

- How would you like to pay? Cash, credit card or check?
- Would you like to pay monthly or quarterly?
- What date do you need it delivered?
- What is the billing address for our records?
- Just give me your OK and it's yours.

The Ben Franklin Close

Salespeople/actors have used this technique for years, having closed many a person leaning on the fence. If properly structured, it can be one of the best tools in your arsenal as to whether or not you are making the right decision.

Whenever Ben Franklin was confronted with a decision, he would take out a piece of paper and place on the heading of the page the words YES and NO. The column with the largest number of check marks gave him the answer he was looking for.

The problem with the way most salespeople/actors use this close is, they will ask you many more leading questions that will inevitably place more checks in the YES column, hence a sale. It's a rigged exercise if you allow yourself to be lead down the primrose path by the salesperson/actor with clever tactics that emotionally manipulate your critical thinking abilities. Remain cautious. Don't allow the "closing of the sale" to proceed without utilizing the Ben Franklin Close on your own.

The basic premise of the Ben Franklin Close is a valid one. Appendix A contains a blank version, allowing you to write your own questions. Appendix B has pre-printed sample relevant questions covering some of the most important financial decisions you may make. Always keep your self-interest in mind. Salespeople/actors are trained not to bring up these types of questions, unless they have no choice.

The two Ben Franklin closing sheets can be enlarged. Making copies for future reference will arm you with the ability to write your own questions for many of your future purchases, in addition to the pre-printed version. Either form will place logic over emotion, thus empowering you, the buyer, with the knowledge needed to benefit your self-interest.

Overcoming Two Different Objectives

Problem: Any buyer's self-interest is themselves and those they care about. A salesperson's self-interest is one and the same for them. "Never the twain shall meet!"

Answer: Working diligently as a team, buyer and seller can provide a "win-win" scenario. On the surface it's quite easy, except human frailty gets in the way. Understanding how to overcome those frailties provides the view to the "winning road." Perhaps the buyer realizes they can afford *only* what they can afford. Perhaps the salesperson decided to *only* work in the interest of the client/customer, even if the commission is less.

Result: Everyone goes home with something. Tomorrow is another day.

The following timeless phrases are relative to the negotiation process. They can serve you well.

"Even Wisdom has to Yield to Self-Interest"

Pindar
Greek Poet
(552 BC - 433 BC)

"Self-Interest: A Concern for One's Own Advantage and Well-Being"

Charles Baudelaire
French Poet
(April 9, 1821 - August 31, 1867)

"Patience is a Virtue"

Ancient Proverbial Phrase

Chapter Seven

The Play Has Ended: Stop, Sit Back, and Relax. Think Critically Before Making a Decision

It's Not Time to Applaud. Pressure is Not in Your Vocabulary
One of the most important phases within the sales process many salespeople/actors utilize to their advantage is pressure. It can be overt or quite subtle, using statements to induce fear of loss such as "today is the last day of the giant sale." Emotion is their friend and logic is their enemy. This is one of your most important critical thinking phases during any sales process, prior to making a final rational decision as to whether you want to sign on the bottom line, or not. The time spent contemplating may very well result in life-changing decisions that could bring personal and financial benefits or consequences to you. Therefore, it's important for your well-being to take this time, whether it be one hour, one day, or whatever is required.

Don't become part of the herd. The decision is yours. Never allow yourself to be pressured.

It's important to understand the entire contract you are contemplating signing. If you do not understand the fine print in the contract, take it to a lawyer or, at the very least, have a knowledgeable person you trust read over the contract before signing.

Should you decide to take a day or two during your critical thinking phase, don't be surprised if the salesperson/actor calls you, possibly trying various sales techniques to convince you they have a *special deal just for you*. If you're really interested in what is being offered, this can be your time to renegotiate, price, terms, and conditions that have been an issue. After all, the salesperson/actor is calling you, not the other way around. Therefore, you are the one in the driver's seat. Use this to your advantage. This time spent is exactly what most salespeople/actors do not want you to do, as they are more concerned for their livelihood, and fear you will decide not to buy, or possibly purchase elsewhere.

You owe your allegiance to making the proper decision only to yourself, as well as those persons you care about. You owe the salesperson/actor absolutely nothing for their time and effort, should you decide the service or product was not in your self-interest. This also includes any immediate family member, or distant relative who happens to be the one trying to sell you. Hence, a good reason for doing business with a stranger, as mixing family and business may not have the result of positive family relations.

To place the occupation of sales in perspective: You are not even thought of as a person to the salesperson/actor, prior to any first initial meeting. You are a *lead*. Upon your first introduction, you have now been elevated from *lead* to *prospect*. Regardless of how *friendly* the salesperson/actor appears in their acting role, they are never your *friend*. Your relationship with them is "Strictly Business." Don't allow yourself to be emotionally led into feeling otherwise. The adversarial reality of your relationship with any salesperson/actor should never be forgotten.

The profession of sales can be correlated to a magician shuffling three balls quickly on a table with slight-of-hand, asking you to tell them which box contains the ball. You can never be certain if what you are hearing is truth or illusion.

The Three Agendas

The agenda of business, public or private, is to make a profit from their product or service, which they are entitled to. The agenda of any salesperson/actor is to earn a commission from the sale of the product or service, as a percentage of that profit, to which they are also entitled. Lastly, the agenda of any consumer is to purchase the product or service, sold by the salesperson/actor, as inexpensively as possible with the best terms and conditions available, which they are entitled to. This scenario is the classic age-old balancing act, of three separate and distinct agendas that have been in play since time immemorial. This tiered natural system automatically creates the following distinct adversarial relationships.

Business vs. Salesperson

Business wants to make a maximum profit by maintaining the lowest overhead as possible, including the smallest commission schedule feasible to their salespeople/actors, while simultaneously building and re-building their sales/acting force, if needed.

Salesperson vs. Consumer

With the salesperson/actor and consumer on the front line, the role of business is to set prices, terms and conditions. The company is now expecting the salesperson/actor to perform to their standards. Interface with the consumer, produce sales at the highest profit possible using tactics designed to produce a "bottom line" positive result that ultimately flows down to the percentage the salesperson/actor receives through their commission schedule.

Therefore, given this business structure, the system dictates you, the consumer to basically fend for yourself. Your only weapon available for you to achieve your "bottom line" is knowledge. K + A = S: <u>Knowledge</u> plus <u>Action</u> equals <u>$uccess.</u>

Ignorance is Bliss - No It Isn't

This is a phrase spoken over many generations, exemplified by Thomas Gray in the eighteenth century from his poem "Ode on a Distant Prospect of Eton College." The last two lines of his poem reads: "No more; where ignorance is bliss, 'tis folly to be wise." Be assured, when dealing with any salesperson/actor, the only ignorance is in the phrase itself. Ignorance of product or service knowledge for that which you are seeking to purchase, is acting in a self-destructive manner.

Researching the product, service, salesperson/actor, and company are critical in order to implement a successful conclusion. Only listening to and believing the salesperson/actor, who has their own personal agenda, adverse to yours, is folly indeed. Over the millennia, too many people have "taken the word" of the salesperson/actor because they *liked* the salesperson, and they wanted to *believe* the sales pitch. These are only some of the reasons why the sales profession has the negative reputation it has so rightly earned. Purchase with wisdom.

Quotes by Albert Einstein that are relative to the sales process.

"It's not that I'm so smart, but I stay with the questions much longer."

"You have to learn the rules of the game, and then, you have to

play better than anyone else."

"We cannot solve our problems with the same thinking that created them."

"Insanity: Doing the same over and over again, and expecting different results."

Albert Einstein
Physicist
(March 14, 1879 - April 18, 1955)

Chapter Eight

Encore!
Asking for Referrals

Congratulations! The play has reached its conclusion. You are fully satisfied and have decided to purchase. The contract is fully understood and signed. You are expecting, as well as being entitled to receive the fruits of your research, and negotiating skills. The barriers between you and the salesperson/actor are down. You think the sales process is finally over. Well, not quite yet. The salesperson/actor is already looking for their next lead, and is hoping you can take them to the promised land of more commissions by means of receiving *free* referrals from you.

You have the power to deliver more commission dollars into the salespersons/actors pocket. After all, this person is now your *friend*. Right! Wrong! This is strictly a business relationship, and you are entitled to some form of compensation for a referral that ends up as a sale. Do not just be a "nice person" by giving away the store. We live in a capitalistic society, and you are entitled to a referral fee for your valuable information. Most sales people will never mention they will remunerate you in some form, unless you ask. It's in their financial interest not to share the wealth, by just continuing to play the role of your *friend*. You have every right to inform them you know how to play the game as well as they do.

A Percentage of Something Beats One Hundred Percent of Nothing

If it is legally appropriate for you to ask for a referral fee, by all means ask. Don't be shy. Specifically, within the financial, insurance, and real estate arena strict laws regarding state and federal licensing are in force. If you are legally licensed, in any of these professional arenas, always complying with federal and state laws, and referral fees are legal, it makes no sense not to ask. You have nothing to lose, and everything to gain. Why should you give away referral names without receiving the proper remuneration you are entitled to receive. The salesperson/actor doesn't give anything away, why should you.

Chapter Nine

Tips on Buying the Most Common Big Ticket Home Items: Think and Buy Only In Your Self-Interest

Purchasing Flooring

1. Maintain Control
Don't let the salesperson talk you into a product you do not need or cannot afford. Know your options.

2. Occupational License and Insurance
Be certain the company and/or the individual doing the installation provides to you, a legal license, the proper amount of liability

insurance, and the assurance the person(s) performing the work are qualified. Make a copy and/or take down the policy number. Take note of the renewal date. Get referrals.

3. Multiple Quotes

Get more than one quote. It's one of the best ways to know if what you are paying is in the ballpark. In addition, this will give you the opportunity to interview multiple vendors for your project regarding the type and quality of the materials needed, as well as determining the professionalism and competence of the vendor(s) you are considering for the job at hand. Become knowledgeable about other product lines offered by various manufacturers.

4. Be Cautious

Always take precautions regarding personal safety, theft, etc. when allowing anyone into your home.

5. How Many Years do You Intend to Live in Your Home?

Utilize an amortization schedule. Determine if the time-frame you intend to live in your new home justifies the initial investment.

6. Read the Guarantee and /or Warranty

Be certain you thoroughly understand the fine print regarding *all* terms and conditions. Just knowing the length of time is insufficient. Specifics such as how repairs and/or returns are accomplished by the vendor or manufacturer are critical, especially for a high valued product. Should there be more than one guarantee and/or warranty, knowledge of knowing the one in first position is critical.

7. Lifestyle Questions
The number of people living in the home (taking every person's wants and needs into consideration), as well as thinking about any pets living in your home, etc. is important to query for the type of product required, from a practical point of view.

8. Maintenance
This is an important issue. Determine your physical and/or financial ability to maintain the product.

9. Use Your Ben Franklin Closing Page

Purchasing Furniture

1. Refer To #1 and #3-#8 by Flooring.

2. Use Your Ben Franklin Closing Page

Purchasing a Heating and Cooling System

1. Refer to #1- #8 by Flooring.

2. Know the Requirements of Your Home
Determine the inside square footage as well as the height of the ceilings. This will help determine the proper size unit needed in order to run efficiently. Also, be certain the air ducts are sufficient to carry a proper air flow throughout your home. Purchasing a unit conducive to the square footage of your home is very important. Should your

home have high cathedral ceilings, the cubic air space must also be taken into consideration. Purchasing a larger system than is required makes no sense and is a waste of money. The salesperson may not inform you of this, as the commission will be larger.

3. Use Your Ben Franklin Closing Page

Purchasing Home Siding and Roofing

1. Refer to #1-#8 by Flooring.

The installer is most definitely a salesperson. This is where the commission money is, even if you are speaking with the person who will be physically performing the installation. The more expensive the product, the larger the "up-charge," that is essentially a commission.

2. Use Your Ben Franklin Closing Page

Purchasing Major Appliances

1. Refer to #1 and #3-#8 by Flooring.

2. Think! What Benefits Do You Expect from Each Appliance

Before Purchasing

- Lifestyle choices that cost additional money
- Glass-top stove versus a standard electric burner/gas

- In-door ice maker with crushed ice capability maker versus no ice maker
- Dishwasher with all the bells and whistles
- Hot water heater storage capacity and rating efficiency

3. Use Your Ben Franklin Closing Page

Chapter Ten

Tips on Buying the Most Common Home Services: Think and Buy Only In Your Self-Interest

Carpenters, Electricians, Plumbers
They can be salespersons as well. Example: *Offering* you a larger hot water heater than you really need. It will initially not only cost you more, but also increase your monthly utility bill.

1. Maintain Control
Don't let the salesperson talk you into a product or service you do not need or cannot afford. Know your options.

2. Occupational License and Insurance
Refer to #2 under Flooring (Chapter Nine)

3. Read the Guarantee and/or Warranty
Refer to #6 under Flooring (Chapter Nine)

4. Multiple Quotes
Refer to #3 under Flooring (Chapter Nine)

5. Be Cautious
Always take precautions regarding personal safety, theft, etc. when allowing anyone into your home.

6. Use Your Ben Franklin Closing Page

Chapter Eleven

Tips on Buying or Leasing Big Ticket Items: Think and Buy Only In Your Self-Interest

Purchasing a New or Used Car

Maintain Control
Don't let the car salesperson talk you into a vehicle that does no fit well into your personal and financial requirements. Drive the vehicle you can comfortably afford, not forgetting normal maintenance costs. Know your options.

Perception vs. Reality

As a matter of culture throughout the years, the car salesperson has always had and probably always will have, the perception of being the ultimate salesperson you should never trust; someone who is almost always willing to gladly sell you a lemon, while laughing all the way to the bank. Because they have the reputation of trying to shake every last dollar from your wallet, (although, in reality, they are no better or worse than salespersons peddling other products or services), it's extremely important to know your game plan before you ever speak with any car salesperson. Most people will tell you they would rather go to the dentist for a root canal than have to deal with a car salesperson, whether purchasing a new or used vehicle. Knowing and maintaining a sound strategy will take the "fear factor" of being "taken to the cleaners" out of the picture.

Lifestyle Questions

It's important to assess your personal needs and desires before you ever think of speaking with any car salesperson. Keep a practical awareness, as it's important to remember purchasing a car means you own a high dollar item that depreciates in value (with some exceptions) as soon as you drive your new or used car off the lot. Questions to consider such as, family size, length of average daily usage, daily mileage requirements, (local vs. highway), how long you intend to own the vehicle, will help make the right decision(s) a positive reality.

Affordability

Should you buy a car you have no financial business owning, you will end up being the loser. The car salesperson will have won the war and collected the commission, having sold you a car you didn't realize you will now struggle to own due to your inability to keep current with the payments, and possibly the up-keep. This reality happens on a daily basis through manipulative sales techniques because the salesperson has duped you into "falling in love" with the vehicle first, before guiding you, in order to determine your ability to comfortably afford the vehicle you desire. Unethical sales techniques are one of the main reasons why the repossession business is as big as it is. In addition, your credit rating just went negative. Thinking critically will determine what type of vehicle you can afford, whether you can or should pay cash, or amortize payments over a number of years. The process of being a "good researcher" deserves your utmost attention, or you may find yourself beginning to *hate* the car you initially *loved*.

Insurance, general maintenance and fuel costs must be major considerations when purchasing a car. Insurance coverage based on insurance industry ratings can be quite pricy on high-end vehicles, including sports cars (whether domestic or foreign). Know your costs before considering any vehicle.

Know Your Price Point and Monthly Payment You Can Afford

Before you see the salesperson, it's imperative you know your budget. You must know the maximum price point and monthly payment you can comfortably afford. NEVER tell the salesperson this information. Giving too much information will place you at a disadvantage, as the salesperson has the ammunition needed to manipulate your emotional wish list by placing you into a car you never had any intention of buying, and may possibly not be able to afford.

Use the vast array of financial calculators available on the internet that will ask you for pertinent information such as price, interest rate, and length of time for the loan. Do not forget you have to have the ability to pay tax, tag and title up front. Know this information prior to ever speaking with a salesperson. Keep it to yourself, or the salesperson may try to "bait and switch" you into another, more expensive car with extended financing that will succumb to what you thought was initially a good deal, but turns into rotten tomatoes. The upgraded vehicle you have now bought may be quite nice, but the extended payments will keep you in debt longer. However, the salespersons commission is larger.

Obtain Financing First - Know the Annual Percentage Rate (APR)

Unless you intend to pay cash, obtain pre-approval from a lending institution with a figure both of you are comfortable with, before you begin your search. It will literally put you in the driver's seat when you find the vehicle you are looking for. Financing from a dealer will most probably add hidden additional costs, fees and the interest rate. It's a major profit center for the dealerships.

It's imperative to know the APR. This is the only true interest rate that really matters. There are almost always two interest rates. The advertised rate the car salesperson may tell you, and the actual APR you may end up with. You must calculate any add-ons you intend to finance by placing them into the equation. You will be unpleasantly surprised how the monthly payment increases. The APR is the rate you are actually paying month-after-month, for the life of the loan. The more you can reduce your costs, the less your monthly payment will be, thus making your payment more affordable, and your life more enjoyable.

Calculate an Affordable Payment

Doing all your homework prior to walking into any showroom is equivalent to being fully armed and loaded for a duel at high noon. The knowledge you can obtain from the financial calculators on the internet, in addition to working with your own banking institution, is priceless. After calculating various price points, interest rates, and monthly time frames, you will know exactly what you can and cannot afford.

Never Allow the Salesperson to Sell You a Car Using the Monthly Payment Scheme

Don't ever present a monthly payment number to the salesperson that you think is affordable. This tactic is the "oldest trick in the book." Upon finding a vehicle you like, insist the salesperson work-up their numbers. Be in charge! You will then have the financial information you have been waiting for to compare and contrast from financial information you have already researched. Utilizing this tactic will develop the right avenue for your smooth financial transition.

History of the Used Car

Anytime you buy a used car it is important to know its history. If you have absolutely no knowledge of the history, you can utilize reliable websites that track every vehicles history, direct from the manufacturer onward to the present time. Questions to consider: Was the vehicle ever in a flood or accident, etc. Read chapter Twenty-Five for websites you can check out.

Manufacturer's Suggested Retail Price (MSRP)

Take a moment to think about that phrase. The manufacturer has *suggested* a retail price. The translation of this well-known phrase is: "We want you to pay as much as possible." It's all about trying to manipulate you into thinking the product is worth, and should sell for what the manufacturer is seeking. The word *suggested* means just that - *suggested,* nothing more. The term "retail price" correlates to paying "full list price." Ignore the MSRP when purchasing a new car.

Present Market Value and Conditions

Be aware of the market value on any car you are considering for purchase. The timing can definitely make a difference, such as a particular week of the month or a specific quarter within the year. All dealers are under the thumb of the manufacturer to produce volume. The overall economy at any given time certainly has a bearing, as well, depending on the public's "likability factor" for a particular vehicle. It's important to be cognizant of the fact the auto dealer and their salespeople view a car, as "just a piece of metal." They will utilize the appropriate tactic from their "bag of tricks" depending on present market/timing conditions, etc. It always comes down to their bottom line profit margin they are under pressure to maintain.

Bells and Whistles

We all love them. The only problem is they cost money. You can count on the salesperson to do their best to emotionally *up-sell* you on as many bells and whistles as possible, as this increases their commission. The added commission for any salesperson has always been the reason for *up-selling* as much as they can. Constantly be aware of the sales techniques bestowed upon you every minute of the sales process. If you're oblivious, you may not know what "hit you" as you are signing your financial life away. Purchase only what you can afford, or walk.

Buying a New Vehicle
Invoice, Rebates, Incentives and Holdbacks

Use the power of the internet for your research. It's invaluable for arming you with knowledge before you walk into the devil's den, otherwise known as the dealer's showroom. The more information you can find out regarding the manufacturer's true wholesale cost to the dealer, as well as any rebates, incentives, and holdbacks, the more leverage you will have during the negotiating process. The real hidden figure can be five percent, or more below the invoice, depending on the vehicles marketability.

Start with the invoice price you already know, due to the homework you have done before stepping into a showroom or onto a car lot to speak with a salesperson. The invoice price, and other listings on websites, allows any dealer room to negotiate. Get whatever information is on the invoice. Many rebates, incentives, and holdbacks the dealer receives from the manufacturer will never appear on the invoice. You may not be able to derive as much information as you would like, especially the holdback percentage, which may be based on the cost overhead while on the dealer's lot. Even if you can't obtain this knowledge, letting the salesperson know you are aware of holdbacks, informs them you do not intend to overpay. You should have plenty of room to negotiate. You will most probably never know the exact total of the manufacturer's incentives to the dealer. Therefore, play hardball and always be prepared to get up and walk out, leaving the salesperson your contact number.

The Finance Office

Don't be duped into thinking when you walk into the finance managers/salespersons office, you have *only* been sent there just to sign the paperwork and leave. The selling continues, regardless of the title placed on the desk. The play is not over yet, *only* your antagonist has changed. "The game is still the same."

Having the advantage of obtaining your financing prior to seeing the salesperson means the finance manager/salesperson has to find other ways to add revenue for the dealership and themselves. Expect a sales pitch for an Auto Protection Insurance Program for loss of income, disability, or death, in addition to a bevy of items from extended warranties to undercoating. If you think any item may be of benefit to you, tell the finance manager/salesperson you want to read the contract on your own time, and you will make a decision within a few days. If you're told it *isn't possible,* and presented with a *one-time offer* requiring you to make a decision on the spot, *stop* and *think critically.* Very few things in life are so important that you must make an immediate decision. Certainly, a car is not one of them. Don't hesitate to tell the finance manager/salesperson you want to check out other dealers before making a decision. You will be amazed at the change in attitude you may see coming in your favor, any time the finance manager/salesperson is concerned you are about to take a walk. They are the last characters you have to deal with, and they "do not" want the deal to go "down the drain."

It's important to remember most items you buy through the finance manager/salesperson can easily be added on to the cost of your car purchase. Therefore, you may now be overpaying for something you don't need, and the monthly payment will increase. Everyone is "making money" except *you*.

Trade-In or Sell on Your Own

Selling your car on your own (if you are willing to be a salesperson), will almost always allow you to end up with more money in your pocket, instead of having the dealer give you as close to wholesale or below, as possible. Flipping your vehicle over to the Used Car Department is money in the bank to the dealer, as they make more on used cars than new ones. Why then, do most people choose to trade-in their vehicle, knowing they could do better? It's a matter of convenience. As with anything else, convenience is not *free*.

Face it, selling a car when you are not in the business is a real hassle. Ads cost money, and it takes time, you may or may not have. The best you can do, should you decide to trade-in to the dealer, is too know by doing your research, how much you ascertain the value of your car to be, and staying focused to get the very best deal.

Should you decide to trade-in your vehicle, knowing you will not receive the same amount of money, had you sold your vehicle privately, does not reflect *one battle lost* means *you cannot win the war.* Consider it a *win* to keep the dealer's profit margin *reasonable,* and that's OK, for they are entitled to a fair return. Never let your guard down, as they can and most probably will gouge your pocketbook as much as they can, while they are shaking your hand, thanking you for your business and referrals.

Buying a Used Vehicle from a Private Owner

First rule to remember when buying a used car from a private owner is they have just taken on the role of car salesperson therefore it's no different than negotiating with a dealer. The relationship is automatically an adversarial one. They want as much as possible for the car, and you want to purchase it as inexpensively as possible.

The only reason anyone buys a product already used, versus new, is obviously to save money. If you are able to find a used car and save between 25% - 40% off the price of a vehicle that is no more than approximately three to five years-old, it may be worth it. Your negotiation process will depend on various factors such as mileage, body condition, year of vehicle, etc.

In order to have a baseline figure to work from, research the current market price of both new and used vehicles. Find the make and model of your choice, including all the bells and whistles. Unless the circumstances are such that you personally know the history of the car, and are satisfied with that knowledge, it's imperative the car be inspected (including the odometer) by a non-partisan mechanic. Costing (on average) $50.00 - $100.00, it may be the cheapest money you will ever spend. If the seller refuses you the option of an independent mechanical inspection, take a walk. It's not worth the risk, no matter how nice the paint job. There may just be something under the hood the owner is hiding. Always ask the seller of the car if there is a manufacturer's warranty, or any other warranty, in force. If so, what is covered, and is it transferable? Otherwise, you are buying the car "as is."

Throughout the entire process, negotiate smart with the owner/salesperson of the car. Should there be any mechanical or body defects found, the vehicle obviously has to be repaired. Otherwise a deduction is in order if you are still interested. Every issue, no matter how small it may seem, is a number that gives you the power to drive the price down. Should you decide the car you want is mechanically sound and physically appealing, but a small price difference remains for a successful sale to occur, remind the owner/salesperson of the additional time spent, and possible cost, for a new classified advertisement. It's a tactic that may change their mind. If there is no "meeting of the minds," leave your phone number. You may just get a call. If a deal is struck, be certain you are receiving a certified clear original title. If you are unsure about the vehicle, and want to know more about it before purchasing, obtain the history of the car, as written previously in this chapter.

Use Your Ben Franklin Closing Page

Leasing vs. Purchasing a New Car

Leasing a car is a double-edged sword. The right answer depends on multiple factors. If your intentions are never to own the car you are leasing, then you want to negotiate as low a selling price as possible on, a vehicle having a high residual value, along with a decent interest rate and low fees. You *must* negotiate these factors the same as when purchasing a car, as well as knowing the APR, length of the lease, and the required down payment. If you are determined to lease instead of buying, shop around. Various cars, dealers, banks, and manufacturers will produce numbers that can be vastly different.

Yes: To Leasing

- The savings of not having to place a down payment of 10% - 20% that could be put to other uses.
- Yearly mileage is not expected to exceed the limits written into the lease, which can be as low as 10,000 miles per year. Should you exceed the yearly lease mileage figure, the charges can become quite steep and it may be a losing proposition at that point to continue driving the car.
- If you have the financial ability to consistently make payments as long as you choose to lease a vehicle, knowing you will never build any equity, leasing can be seen as a lifestyle benefit by having another new car when the old lease expires. The time frame is usually one to three years.
- Leasing provides the advantage of never being concerned about repairs.

- Leasing a car can be less expensive if it's been subsidized by the manufacturer.

No: To Leasing

- Driving over the number of yearly miles can be expensive. Be aware of the limitations. You can purchase additional miles as insurance, which is generally paid up front.
- Should you decide you want to exit the lease prior to the contract, an early termination fee is normally included in when leasing.
- If your lifestyle is such that you have always owned and been satisfied maintaining a car for a number of years, after paying it off, leasing may not be your cup of tea. You may not like the fact leasing payments never stop. If you think your present vehicle is drivable with little repair for the near future, and you are right, then you would have saved yourself possibly thousands of dollars in lease payments.
- If the monthly payments are structured higher than they should be, due to dealer manipulation methods such as increasing the base price, etc., then leasing is not a good deal, even if the monthly leasing number fits into your budget. Should this become the case, you are overpaying each and every month, while the dealer has taken their profit and the car salesperson has collected their commission.

Use Your Ben Franklin Closing Page

Purchasing a New Boat

Read Tips on Buying a New and Used Car. There are many aspects to the purchase of a car that you can duplicate in regards to a boat. Taking time to read the section on cars will help you familiarize with many of the same questions and issues when purchasing a boat.

Lifestyle Considerations
When purchasing a boat, the importance of taking into account your lifestyle must be of high priority. Because there are so many different types of boats, serving many purposes, know your objective(s) and be certain the type of boat you buy will serve your particular needs. Are you only interested in deep sea fishing? Or, do you just want to cruise along the river, or both?

Water Safety
Safety must be a serious consideration when boating, just as it is when driving your car. However, driving a boat on the water places you in a very different mode of transportation. Contact the U.S. Coast Guard, as they are the definitive authority on the subject of boating.

Warranties
When buying as a package from a dealer, be certain the warranty covers both the boat and the engine(s). They are two separate pieces of equipment, and must be listed as such, with a serial number(s) and a Hull Identification Number (HIN).

Know Your Boat
It's very important to know the weight, horsepower and passenger capacity of any boat you are purchasing. If your vessel is under 20 feet, check on the flotation standard in the event of an emergency. Know the criteria about the venting system, electrical requirements, and the fuel operating system.

Insurance

Protect all your assets, on land and in the water. Be certain to buy Protection and Indemnity Coverage in the event of an injury or claim. Events can happen that are unpredictable. Imagine having invited your "best friend(s)" out onto your boat for a nice relaxing day on the water, only to end up defending yourself against a lawsuit because an accident or injury occurred. Unfortunately, there are no *friends* when the subject of money comes into play.

Purchasing a Used Boat

When buying a used boat, the same basic common sense rules apply as they do when buying a used car. A certified marine mechanic or surveyor, working solely for you, can advise you in making the right decision to purchase or not. The answer may be purchasing the vessel with the required repairs paid for by the seller, or possibly a reduction in price. Seek out a certified marine mechanic paid for by you, who will be looking out for your best-interest.

Use Your Ben Franklin Closing Page

Chapter Twelve

Tips on Buying Real Estate: Think and Buy Only In Your Self-Interest

**National Association of Realtors ®
Code of Ethics**
For a century, members of this organization have maintained a strict code of ethics for the real estate agent/salesperson(s), known specifically, as Realtors®, to subscribe to a strict code of ethics. The code provides their clients with the highest degree of professionalism, ethics and service. It's important to know not all real estate licensees are required to belong to the organization.

It is most certainly commendable the NAR had the foresight, and continues to maintain such a high standard. Should you choose to purchase and/or sell property, it may behoove you to seek a real estate agent/salesperson who is a member of this prestigious organization. There are a multitude of industries, national and multinational that should seriously considering following this moral avenue.

Caveat Emptor: Always keep in mind, as exemplary as any organizations By-Laws and/or Code of Ethics are written, base elements of human nature can and will rear their ugly head. Remain cautious when speaking with all salespersons. Let history be your guide.

Purchasing Residential Property
Maintain Control

Should you decide to use the services of a real estate agent/salesperson, don't let them talk you into a home that does not fit your lifestyle, or your pocketbook. Know your options. Bring up all your antennas and take a hard look at the real estate/salesperson who will be "working for you." This will be one of your best or worst experiences in your life. Being selective by your choosing the *ethical* real estate/salesperson working to fulfill your wants and needs is critical. Take another hard look at the real estate/salesperson showing you homes. Ask yourself: Is this person(s) truly competent in their field, working in my self-interest? Should you think the answer to be yes, then you are off to the races, otherwise, keep searching for proper representation.

Location, Location, Location

Location should be upper-most in your mind when searching for the home of your dreams. One of the most difficult decisions you must make when buying the home you are going to live in, is keeping the emotion of the purchase in check. The more you are able to separate emotion from logic regarding one of the most important purchases in your life, the greater your emotional happiness will be when you move in.

Look Up Comparable Sales

If you're working with a real estate agent/salesperson they can do it for you. Otherwise, you can get the information yourself through the internet by bringing up the tax assessors/appraisers website for the county you have an interest in. Should they not have a website, go to an appraiser's office in person. There are also a number of commercial websites that can provide valuable market information.

Pre-Approval - Don't Put the Cart in Front of the Horse

Obtaining a pre-approval for a mortgage, prior to your search, is prudent. It will put you in the driver's seat when you find the property you are looking for.

Paying Cash vs. Obtaining a Mortgage

If you're fortunate enough to have the financial ability to pay cash for your home, and save yourself many thousands of dollars in interest, you will definitely be able to "call the shots." One important consideration and possible future advantage for paying cash are unforeseen events, such as loss of income through work or investments that could result in you not being able to meet your mortgage. Take a hard look at your personal situation prior to making that crucial decision, and proceed accordingly. Regardless of the method you choose, use caution. Think critically! You will be protecting your future, your home, and your nest egg.

Negotiate with the Real Estate Agent

Should you have no choice but to work with a real estate agent/salesperson, and the price negotiations are not enough to bring forth a meeting of the minds, then do the *unthinkable*. Tell the real estate agent/salesperson (with tact) to reduce the commission. If the property is listed with a real estate agent/salesperson, your real estate agent/salesperson can very easily have a discussion with their office, or another if required. If all involved want the sale badly enough, the parties can have a "meeting of the minds," reduce the commission percentage that will satisfy buyer and seller, and still make a profit to which they are entitled. It's important to know that "nothing is written in stone," although not all real estate agents/salespersons will willingly bring up the subject because it's commission money out of their pocket. However, it can be accomplished through smart negotiation on your part.

Note: If you must use a real estate agent/salesperson, investigate with the state or local real estate board for any possible complaints or issues against the real estate agent/salesperson and/or the brokerage firm.

For Sale by Owner

The first rule to remember when buying a home from a private owner: They have just taken on the role of owner/salesperson. Therefore, it's no different than negotiating with a real estate agent/salesperson from the "other side." The relationship is automatically an adversarial one. They want as high a figure as they can possibly get for the home, and you want to purchase it as inexpensively as possible.

If you have the knowledge and ability to purchase a home without the assistance of a real estate agent/salesperson, do it. You can save on the average 3% - 7% of the *up-charge*, due to the commission the owner must pay to the real estate company for the listing. Always seek out "For Sale by Owner," as this can give you the advantage of not having to pay for the real estate agent/salespersons commission. This may take extra "leg work," such as obtaining information about schools, public transportation, shopping, etc. The time spent may possibly save you thousands of dollars you can put in your pocket to spend on decorating your new home, or perhaps place into an investment product. All-in-all, it certainly beats seeing the commission money fly right out the window, never to return.

Lifestyle Questions
Before you purchase, think and ask yourself questions such as how you plan to live in your new home. For example:

- Are you looking for a home until the kids are gone, and then expect to sell, or would the home meet your needs with only you and/or your significant other living there?
- Are you more interested in purchasing with the intent of making a profit at resale?
- Over and above the mortgage, think about the monthly/yearly upkeep. Taxes, insurance, heating and air conditioning costs, as well as general maintenance, must all be taken into consideration. Can you realistically maintain some things yourself? Will your future income be enough to meet these obligations?

Property Inspection
The cheapest money you can spend, prior to purchase, should be written as a contingency in the purchase and sale contract. Insist on a required inspection by a qualified/certified inspector of your choosing, paid by and working for you. The money spent for an inspector is a drop in the bucket when compared to the cost and aggravation of any problems you could incur that you were not aware of, and maybe

not told about by the owner, as they have taken on the role of salesperson. Your home may be your palace, but it's also your investment. Protect it!

Final Inspection Scenarios

- **The home is perfect:** This is very doubtful. Every home has a problem, no matter how small it may be. However, the issue(s) brought up by the inspector are quite minor and do not concern you, based on the price of the home.
- **The home has issues:** They have to be dealt with. Either the owner takes care of the problem(s), or you negotiate the issue(s).
- **The insurmountable problem(s):** Too difficult and/or expensive to correct therefore, it's time to walk.

Use your Ben Franklin Closing Page

Purchasing Commercial Property
Maintain Control
Don't let the real estate agent/salesperson talk you into a property that does not meet your financial objectives. Know your options.

Location, Location, Location
Extremely important: In order to meet your financial objectives.

Dealing With a Real Estate Agent/Salesperson
The odds are probably better than 50% a real estate agent/salesperson is going to be involved with a commercial property. Be certain

you are working with a person who has the knowledge required to operate in this specialized arena. Depending on the price (which can run into the millions), you should make it SOP (Standard Operating Procedure) and have the real estate/salespersons commission become a part of the negotiation. There is no affair of the heart when it comes to buying or selling commercial property. It's strictly a business investment.

Note: If you must use a real estate agent/salesperson, investigate with the state or local real estate board and/or use any websites listed in chapter twenty-five for any possible complaints or issues against the real agent/salesperson and/or the brokerage firm.

Know Your Exit Strategy Before you Purchase

- How long do you intend to hold onto the property?
- Do you want to own the property throughout your lifetime and leave it to your heirs?
- Do you want to sell the property as soon as you can realize a comfortable profit potential?
- Do you want to utilize the possible value in a 1031 exchange?
- Do you want a buy-in investor in the future?
- Do you want to refinance, and take out whatever equity has been built up? This strategy can give you additional capital for other projects.

Does the Deal Make Sense?

Unless the deal makes financial sense and accomplishes your goals from a lifestyle viewpoint, it may not serve your self-interest to go any further. Walk, and go on to the next project.

Property Inspection

The cheapest money you can spend prior to purchasing commercial property, which must be written as a contingency in the purchase and sale agreement, is the inspection by a qualified/certified commercial property inspector of your choosing, paid by and working for you. The lending institution may insist on it. The money spent for an inspector is miniscule when compared to the cost and aggravation of any future problems that could arise.

Use Your Ben Franklin Closing Page

Chapter Thirteen

Tips on Obtaining a Mortgage: Think and Buy Only In Your Self-Interest

Purchasing a Residential or Commercial Mortgage

Maintain Control
Don't let the mortgage broker, mortgage banker, or bank representative talk you into a mortgage you cannot afford to maintain. Remember, they are all salespersons, so know your options.

Cash or Mortgage
The odds are you will obtain financing. When buying a commercial property, it's rare to pay cash, for its leverage most investors are seeking in order to fulfill the bottom line.

Residential purchases can be quite different, depending on the buyer's needs and wants. When you have found the piece of property you have been searching for, unless you intend to pay cash, you must obtain a mortgage. If the financing isn't beneficial to meet your requirements, you will either begin to detest the home you are living in, or, if it's a commercial property, you will realize little or no return. Unforeseen issues can come up after you sign the purchase and sale agreement, before financing is approved. Always line up your ducks by obtaining financing first, when applicable, so there are no undesirable surprises that may make it difficult or impossible to purchase.

Interest Rate - Know the Annual Percentage Rate

It is imperative to know the APR. This is the only true interest rate that really matters. There are almost always two rates. The initial rate you were first told about and the rate due to the *fees* various salespeople will add into the purchase price as front-end and back-end commissions. Calculate the actual APR you will be paying, with all the costs to know the actual amortized monthly cost for the life of the loan.

The only weapon in your arsenal is the *art of negotiation*. The more you can reduce the phony *fees,* which are nothing more than pure, upfront profit, the more you will retain financially. The less your APR is, the lower and more affordable you mortgage will be.

Fees - AKA/ Commissions

By any other name, a *fee* is a commission going to persons known and unknown by you. Some of the pseudonyms, used by professionals in place of the word *commission* are:

- Application Fee
- Closing Fee
- Lender Fee

- Origination Fee
- Points
- Processing Fee
- Settlement Fee
- Recording Fee

Don't Stop Negotiating
Use your negotiating skills to reduce or eliminate as many *fees* as possible. Dealing with mortgage brokers, mortgage bankers, or bank representatives is (in reality) confronting a *salesperson*. The more they can tack onto your loan, the more commission they make at your expense. When working with any of the personnel relative to financing during and after the purchasing process, always remember: There is no legal law stating you cannot negotiate down the *fees, points, etc.* on either side. "Nothing is written in stone." Never assume it cannot be done, for it can, depending on the many various market conditions at that time.

The Person Sitting Across the Desk is a Salesperson
They may refer to themselves as a mortgage broker, mortgage banker or originator. However, their real occupation is in sales. You can be assured they receive a commission based on *fees* and *points,* added into your mortgage. They're the *middlemen* in the transaction. It's not their money they are lending. They take your information, *shop* your mortgage, find a lender, *sell* the mortgage, and collect a commission.

Reading with a fine tooth comb, the Good Faith Estimate and Federal Truth in Lending Disclosure Statement, is where the "rubber meets the road." Reading and dissecting the figures appropriately will definitely let you know all commissions, front-end and back-end, giving you the needed information to calculate the APR.

You generally have a better opportunity to save yourself some money, if you can work directly with a bank. If the bank or credit union is a "portfolio lender," they lend, and maintain, what they write. If it's not possible to obtain a mortgage directly from a portfolio lender, you may still save yourself some commission money by dealing directly with a reputable bank or credit union.

Regardless of the title the person you are speaking with has on their business card or on their desk, they are a salesperson out for every dollar they can squeeze out of you. Use your negotiating skills with any mortgage broker, mortgage banker, or bank representative to reduce the *fees* and *points*. Never assume it cannot be done. Always negotiate. Market conditions and competition always apply.

Making Sense of Different Mortgage Programs
Depending on your "game plan," each and every mortgage has a different strategy.

Fixed Rate - Fifteen or Thirty Year
How long do you intend to own the property? You can save yourself thousands of dollars if you pay off your mortgage in fifteen years. The difference in the payment is not that great and well worth the cost. If you are concerned about the difference, you can take out a thirty year mortgage and pay the difference each month you feel comfortable doing so. Perform your due diligence, and be certain there is no pre-payment penalty. If you are eligible, look into a VA (Veteran's Administration) or an FHA (Federal Housing Administration) mortgage.

Adjustable Mortgage Rate (ARM)
How much of a "risk taker" are you? Can you sleep well knowing your mortgage rate could change periodically, based on factors over which you have no control? If this is an issue, and you're going to get an ulcer over it, then going fixed may be the answer. If that's the case, you now have to consider whether a fifteen or thirty-year mortgage serves your self-interest.

Interest Only w/Re-Amortization Clause and Amortized Mortgage w/Balloon
These two specific mortgages generally serve the purpose of a well-informed investor, and are rare for the residential homeowner.

Interest only w/re-amortization will, at some point, require the principal to be paid or the loan could be refinanced. If neither of these options is preferred, the only other choice is to place the property on the market for resale.

Amortized mortgage w/balloon payment mortgages generally amortize the payments on a thirty year period. However, the entire balance is due and payable on the balloon date.

Obtaining a Legitimate Current Market Appraisal
Be certain the appraisal of the property is a legitimate market-based document. You don't want to obtain a mortgage for a piece of property (residential or commercial) that is not valued at a current market price.

Note:
If you must use a mortgage broker/mortgage banker/originator/salesperson, investigate with your state board and/or use websites listed

in chapter twenty-five for any possible complaints or issues against them and/or the brokerage firm.

Use Your Ben Franklin Closing Page

Purchasing a Reverse Mortgage

Reverse Mortgages vs. Standard Mortgage

Any person who owns a home and is 62 years of age, or older, is generally eligible for a reverse mortgage. Before anyone leaps for the *benefits* pitched by salespeople, AKA Counselors, be certain you understand to the fullest, *all* the terms and conditions of the mortgage.

A reverse mortgage is *exactly* the opposite of a standard mortgage. The amount of capital a reverse mortgage provides is money in your bank account, tied to numerous rules and regulations. You may have the option of receiving a lump sum or being paid in installments. On the surface it sounds as if it's for everyone age 62 or older. That's hardly the case. As with anything else, you must understand the benefits and consequences of the program.

Reverse mortgages were designed for elderly people who intend to stay in their home until they die. Period! If you are considering a reverse mortgage, this is your first and foremost caveat. Should you decide sometime in the future, you would like to sell your home and move to another location, the mortgage must be satisfied. In addition, there must be no liens on the property. Reverse mortgages definitely serve a purpose, as long as you know *exactly* what the end result will be, and it will serve your agenda.

A reverse mortgage can be used as a piggy bank to supplement your retirement years any way you wish. Essentially what a reverse mortgage achieves is the ability to tap into the equity of your home without the need to repay during your lifetime.

It is not the intent of this book to say *yea* or *nay* to any reverse mortgage program. It's a very personal financial decision to be made by any homeowner who is considering one. The issue is two-fold: Understanding the program in full, and the salesperson trying to get you to sign your name on the application, may lead to your signing your home away. "The Devil is in the Details." Should you be considering a reverse mortgage, perform total "due diligence" before making a decision. The benefit or consequence of that decision could have a profound effect on your well-being for the balance of your life.

Reverse mortgages have many fees applied that fatten the wallet of the salesperson. You must know *all* costs for the reverse mortgage. Never forget, many are *negotiable*.

Seek expert advice with someone you trust. There are many excellent websites, on this subject. Look up chapter twenty-five for a sampling. Ask the same question, as written in chapter twelve: Is the person(s) representing the mortgage company, truly competent in their field working in my self-interest?

Use Your Ben Franklin Closing Page

Chapter Fourteen

Tips on Buying Intangibles: Think and Buy Only In Your Self-Interest

Purchasing an Annuity
Maintain Control
Don't let the annuity agent/salesperson talk you into an annuity not designed for you. Know your options.

Annuities are Unique Individual Contracts
Most annuities are purchased through insurance companies. Therefore, your first thought is the financial strength of the company to which you are handing over your money. Feeling *satisfied* with the company is not enough, for as you investigate the product line

offered you may find out nothing meets your needs. Should that be the case, it makes no sense, to buy an annuity from that particular company, even if you have an insurance policy(s) with them, and your favorite relative (or best friend) just happens to be the annuity agent/salesperson.

Because there are so many different types of annuities, doing your research before you purchase is imperative. Take as long as you must to obtain the knowledge needed for the right decision, as this could very well have a profound effect on *your* future financial well-being, as well as the financial well-being of other persons named in the annuity.

Know Your Needs Regarding the Annuity that Matches Your Goals

Are you looking for a lifetime payout or a payout for only for a certain period of time? Are you setting up the annuity only for yourself or is there going to be a joint survivor clause included in the contract for a spouse, or other heirs you have an interest in? Be certain to fill out a "suitability form," required by legitimate insurance companies and their agent/salespersons. See chapter twenty-five for some listed websites that can provide you with the information needed in order for you to make a rational decision.

A Highly Regulated Industry

When speaking with an annuity agent/salesperson, it's important to know how highly regulated the business is. Only authorized literature from the company is allowed, as state agencies control all compliance regulations. Any annuity agent/salesperson preying on people with unlawful literature, and/or false or misleading sales tactics can lose their license.

Internet and Mail Solicitation

Annuities can be as varied as life insurance policies, each serving a different purpose, Therefore, before you jump into the annuity fire because you received a beautifully designed, glossy four-color brochure, or clicked on an equivalent website that promised you a world of luxury in your golden years, it would be prudent to speak with a professional, *ethical* annuity agent/salesperson, working only in your best-interest. A professional who can intelligently and methodically provide you with the information needed to make a rational decision. There are many different types of annuity products, each designed for a particular purpose. The following definitions are for most basic annuities are:

- **Fixed Annuity** - The payments will remain the same, as in a CD (certificate of deposit) written in the contract for the life term of the annuity which can vary depending on the particular annuity.
- **Variable Annuity** - This annuity will give you the option of participating in the stock market or other forms of investments. The draw is the *possibility* of greater returns. The key word is *possibility*. The downside that exists is premium and interest money can be lost. Choices made can be conservative or aggressive, and can generally be changed, as stated in the terms of the annuity prospectus. This type of annuity is not for the faint-of-heart, having been designed for the sophisticated purchaser. Extremely careful consideration must be considered before signing into this type of annuity.
- **Immediate Annuity** - The insurance company receives only one payment, after which a specific amount of income is distributed within a stipulated time frame, usually six months to one year. A payout can be for a certain period of time, or a lifetime.
- **Single Premium Deferred Annuity** - Payments for this type of annuity generally start years down the road. The period of accumulating the money required to fund the annuity can take a number of years, after which, a specified time can be chosen to begin receiving payments. This annuity can function as a 401K, and can be structured multiple ways, depending on the risk adversity of the policyholder.

- **Multiple Premium Deferred Annuity** - Similar to a Single Premium Deferred Annuity with the exception of multiple payments over a specified time.
- **Equity Index Annuity** - This annuity is usually structured in segments of percentage secured as being fixed with a portion invested in the market, or a variable combination of both. The sell on this type of annuity is the *floor*. The annuity can never lose any value below the "floor value," and may increase if the market goes up. Risk assessment must be considered with this type of annuity.

Read the Prospectus

Upon making what you think appears to be a good fit, the next logical step is to read and understand the prospectus of the specific annuity under consideration. The real terms, conditions, etc. are always in the prospectus. This is where the "rubber meets the road." Almost all companies selling annuities have glossy four color marketing material. The marketing brochures are designed to induce you emotionally into purchasing an annuity, usually with photos of people leisurely fishing or sunbathing on some far-away beach. While the scenes are inviting, never rely on the four-color process photos, or the language in the brochure, to give you an overview of the annuity. The prospectus is the *only* document that truly matters for you to be able to make an informed decision as to whether or not, a specific annuity is going to meet your self-interest.

If reading the prospectus appears to be too daunting, find a second neutral party who has the ability to understand the *fine print* and mathematical calculations, in order to be absolutely certain the annuity meets your needs. If it does not, it's time to move on with your research, whether it is with the same or different company, or perhaps another annuity agent/salesperson. If you purchase an annuity that eventually does not meet your needs, you have no recourse but to live with it. It's a contract! Meanwhile, the annuity agent/salesperson has collected their commission.

One major reason to purchase an annuity is for the comfort of knowing the payout will continually flow throughout your lifetime, and the lifetime of your heirs, if that option has been exercised. If the annuity is a 401K, the interest is tax deferred by federal law, until you begin receiving a payout, unless it's a Roth annuity, meaning the taxes are paid up-front.

Required Minimum Distribution (RMD)
Should you have a traditional 401K or IRA, you must begin to withdraw funds by April 1st of the year following the year you turn 70 1/2. It's imperative you understand this when signing up. This is the time the correct choice for your needs and wants must take primetime consideration. Be certain to obtain the proper financial advice from a competent person. Check with the IRS for any possible exceptions.

Your' Agenda vs. the Insurance Company's Agenda
Purchasing an annuity (depending on the type) is basically a *bet* with the insurance company. You want to outlive the value of your policy, and begin living off their money. This can be a real bargain if you outlive the mortality tables. Of course, the insurance company is betting the opposite. The sooner you and/or your spouse or heirs die (if that protection is included in the policy), the more lucrative the policy will be to the company.

Ask Questions and Find the
Right Annuity Agent/Salesperson
Purchasing an annuity is an investment that requires much thought before taking the plunge. Each product stands on its own merits. Therefore, depending on your future lifestyle, financial needs or those of a spouse or other person to whom financial security is

important to you, the correct decision is critical. The purchase of an annuity is equivalent to standing in front of a buffet table. Only choose the options you want, but choose carefully, as there is no recourse with an annuity after the "free look" period (which is generally thirty days, depending on state laws). After that, you have to live with it, which means it is literally a lifetime-making decision.

Asking the right questions and getting the correct answers is the daunting part of the process. Depending on the annuity agent/salesperson, receiving the necessary answers pertaining to your specific needs can be a most difficult and time-consuming exercise. Should you not be receiving intelligent, provable answers to your questions, do not waste time with the annuity agent/salesperson you are speaking with, even if you think the insurance company is a solid financial institution that can meet your financial objectives, locate another annuity agent/salesperson, (having no regrets) with the same and/or different, insurance company and start over at square one. It is imperative you understand your contract is with the insurance company, not with the annuity agent/salesperson. They both know it, therefore to the insurance company it make absolutely no difference who the annuity agent/salesperson of record is, other than being properly licensed and appointed. Buying an annuity can be a tedious process. However, there are no shortcuts when making a lifetime decision that will tie up your money the way an annuity can.

One stock sales technique to watch out for is any annuity agent/salesperson telling you they will always be there for you. You have just heard a line from Sales 101. There are two distinct flaws in this ridiculous statement:

- The annuity agent/salesperson may pre-decease you.
- The annuity you may be considering, or have bought, is not with the annuity agent/salesperson. It's with the insurance company. Once you own it, your financial relationship is exclusively with the company. The most any annuity agent/

salesperson can hope for is a referral, and/or possibly another product.

Owning an annuity can be an excellent part of your financial planning if the right product with the right company is chosen. An annuity must be purchased knowing exactly what the ups and downs are, and can be a terrific investment that can carry you through your lifetime and/or the lifetime of those persons important to you. There is no one perfect annuity. The *fine print* in the prospectus will let you know if it meets your needs. One very important component to most annuities is looking for the most critical benefits that are important to you. Purchasing an annuity with benefits added that are of no interest to you will only increase your cost, and could marginally decrease the critically important primary benefits. No annuity is going to give you a benefit without a cost, which is one of many reasons why it's important to studiously research your needs and ask questions before making a decision. This will allow you to control the decision-making process regarding the built-in costs. It makes no sense to purchase an option you don't value.

The following list of questions present some of the most important asked to the annuity agent/salesperson. They must be correctly answered to your satisfaction in order to properly work through this critical financial decision that can have a positive or negative impact on your future as well as your loved ones.

- How long has the insurance company been in business?
- What is the financial strength rating of the company?
- What are the fees/management services/administrative charges in the policy? These costs are in addition to the commission earned by the insurance agent/salesperson, and must be considered, as they will be an important part in determining the future payout.
- What is the accumulated interest rate, and how is it calculated?
- Over what period of time is the annuity guaranteed? Every annuity has a different objective, depending on your specific needs.

- Does the annuity have spousal protection, if desired, as well as protection for contingency person(s)? Always be aware, spousal protection will reduce the payout if you are older than your spouse.
- At what age will the annuity be accessible to begin receiving a payout? The calculation of the value at a specific age, at a specified time period, will determine the actual amount of payout.
- Is there a "free look" period and, if so, how long?
- What is the rate of interest? Is it simple or compounded? How are the calculations set?
- How much life insurance protection is locked into the annuity, if any?

Use Your Ben Franklin Closing Page

Purchasing Life Insurance

Maintain Control
Don't let the insurance agent/salesperson talk you into a policy not designed for you. Know your options.

A Highly Regulated Industry
Life insurance, as with annuities, is also highly state regulated including the insurance agent/salesperson, literature, etc. In defense of any insurance agent/salesperson many people think they can automatically buy life insurance less expensively on the internet, or through the mail. It's important to know just how highly regulated the financial industry is from federal to state agencies. Discounts and/or rebates are illegal. The only variance in price is what each company decides to charge. Many insurance brokers give themselves fancy names and/

or titles, trying to get you to think they can provide you with a lower price not available through other agencies and/or brokers. It's critical to always keep in mind that price is not the only factor. The financial rating and strength of any insurance company is just as important. Given this fact, working with a reputable insurance agent/salesperson is paramount to your self-interest, IF they function in a consistent, *ethical* manner, maintaining your needs first.

When you are in the market for life insurance, it's advisable to thoroughly read the previous section about annuities, as there is a synergy between the two products. One major difference between an annuity and most life insurance policies, with the possible exception of whole life, is the annuities are specifically designed to provide a payout to you while you and/or your spouse are living, with the secondary benefit of leaving a legacy. Therefore, you must ask questions that pertain specifically to different types of life insurance policies relative to your specific needs. While you are living is the time to think and ask about the following variables:

Lifestyle - Occupation - The type of lifestyle you lead, as well as your occupation regarding any hazards that may be involved, should be a prime concern to you. Realizing that on any given day you, being the income provider, may not be alive to provide a livelihood for those persons you care about, is reason enough to want to maintain a specific standard of living for them.

Future Financial Goals and Needs - Policies that provide cash when needed for reasons such as: A down payment for a worthwhile purpose, college tuition, or unexpected expenses.

Internet, Mail Solicitation and Public Relations Material

There are many insurance policies that have different names, most of which are a variation of the three basic policies listed below, each serving a different purpose, Therefore, before you jump into the fire because you received a beautifully designed four-color brochure, or clicked on an equivalent website that promised what may appear as the specific product possessing all the bells and whistles you are looking for and want, consider the following. Speak with a professional, *ethical* life insurance agent/salesperson working for your interests, who can intelligently and methodically provide you with the information needed in order to make a rational decision.

Whole Life Insurance - The most comprehensive and highest premium cost, due to the guarantee of a death benefit and cash growth that has a guaranteed rate of interest, with level premiums throughout the life of the contract.

Universal Life Insurance - This type of policy is a cousin to Whole Life, with some very important changes that provide flexibility to the policyholder who does not want to incur a set schedule normally required to pay the premium. This type of policy can function quite well if the policyholder understands responsibility. The premiums, death benefit, and any cash values are dependent on how much, and when, a premium is paid. A fee/commission is charged to the policy on a periodic schedule, which can always be viewed, thereby allowing a policyholder to immediately know the present value at any point in time so they can make changes accordingly.

Term Life Insurance - Many people buy term because it's the least expensive. Term policies are designed for a specific number of years, generally ending with a maximum of twenty years, after which the policy can sometimes be extended with upgraded premiums, or terminated. The premiums, number of years, and death benefit are fixed.

Do Not Forget: Looking to purchase an annuity or life insurance can be one of the most important decisions in your life. Ask the very same questions of those salespersons, as you would of the ones who sell real estate and mortgages. You are always looking for *competency* and *ethics*.

Use Your Ben Franklin Closing Page

Funerals - The Final Purchase

Maintain Control
Should you have the foresight to purchase a life insurance policy, keeping everyone informed as to what your final wishes are, you are providing the knowledge and satisfaction to yourself and your heirs the benefit of additional financial and emotional distress as to their future after your death. Otherwise, it is entirely possible the funeral director/salesperson may talk your heirs into a funeral with all the extras that may not be affordable, and not designed for what you would have preferred. If cremation was the known choice based on previous discussions, you can prevent the funeral director/salesperson from talking your heirs into a full burial that will cost more. Knowing and controlling through pre-planning your options in advance will allow you piece of mind, and your loved ones the opportunity to control the type of funeral desired that can also make a substantial financial difference to all surviving person(s).

Taking Advantage of Your Emotions
The purchase of a funeral is, understandably, one of the most difficult emotional situations anyone will ever be confronted with. The devastation of losing a loved one, especially when it's unexpected, is precisely what the funeral industry relies on in order to maximize profits, as the funeral industry is not unlike any other profit making enterprise: *It's all about the money.* The funeral director/salesperson is an actor presenting their best believable performance. Should you tell the funeral director/salesperson you don't have the funds for your loved ones funeral, expect an immediate change in attitude, as the phony mask of concern comes off.

Pre-Plan the Inevitable

No one, regardless of wealth or station, can avoid death. If wealthy people could avoid the inevitable, they would be doing it all the time. The ancient Egyptians thought they could at least cheat death by taking their physical possessions with them. The buying of a product, known as a funeral, is the last thing you may want to think about or be confronted with. However, given the fact death is unavoidable, the subject must be considered.

A lack of logic can happen to anyone at a difficult time, and the emotions of guilt and fear can cause the surviving person(s) to overspend, and possibly arrange the very opposite of what the deceased would have preferred. Therefore, the wise thing to do is pre-plan, knowing your own wishes will be met, and the financial stability of loved ones left behind will not be abused. The advantage of pre-planning provides the deceased, and the survivor with peace of mind the funeral expenses are paid for, alleviating survivors from having to think about money when overwhelmed with grief. It will provide the "peace of mind" you will need for one of life's most painful moments.

The Two Most Common Methods of Pre-Planning

Final Expense Life Insurance Policy - Sold as "final expense," these policies are generally a graded-down version of whole life with smaller payouts. Should you wish to purchase a final expense policy, it should be noted you may still have to medically qualify. If not, it's possible to purchase a modified version that does not provide the full benefit for an average of two years after purchase. Shop around, ask questions, and be certain the policy is transferable to the funeral home where you think your final arrangements will be made, especially if they are out-of-state. With the age of the country increasing, the insurance companies are targeting this market full steam ahead.

Funeral Trust - A trust can be opened with a bank, an insurance company, or with some funeral homes. One of the most important things to investigate when entering into a trust is, the trust itself. Questions regarding reputation, financial stability, and the ability to transfer a funeral to the location of choice, at time of need, (including out-of-state) are just some of the important items on your agenda prior to purchase. Shop around, just as you would when purchasing life insurance or an annuity.

Pre-Plan for the Inevitable or Face the Consequences

Choosing not to have a plan may very well present your survivor with immediate decisions they may not be financially prepared for. This disadvantage can place a surviving person in a most difficult, stressful situation that is emotionally stressful enough at the outset. Emotional disarray is what a funeral director/salesperson looks for. *It's money in the bank*. The funeral industry has a long, well-documented negative history when it comes to taking advantage of the person(s) surviving the deceased.

One major difference between buying a car, and buying a funeral, is that most people never think about shopping around for a funeral until the time arrives. Many surviving person(s) feel intense pressure and/or guilt as they are being pitched for an ostentatious funeral the deceased person never anticipated. Be aware: The funeral director/salesperson views the selling of a funeral, and any extras they can conjure up in your mind, as profit. It's a business. Period! The only difference is the product. Therefore, don't be afraid to negotiate, whether you are arranging your funeral in advance or making arrangements for a loved one who is deceased.

Should you suspect you are being pressured and not receiving all proper disclosures, tell the funeral director/salesperson you intend to report their improper representation to the FTC/Federal Trade Commission. This will most definitely get their attention. Take a walk if you must, just as you would in a car dealership. They may stop you at the door try to smooth things over, and re-negotiate.

Otherwise, have the funeral performed with another funeral company. Research in advance and have a plan.

The need to purchase a funeral for a deceased person is obviously a very different and difficult emotional purchase that may, to make matters worse, be totally unexpected. Surviving person(s) generally want to do right by the deceased, but may be too wrought with sorrow to think straight. They are the perfect target for the funeral director/salesperson to up-sell everything at a time when emotions are probably "running high." In the eyes of the funeral director/salesperson, what better time to *up-sell* a "better casket" or "finer flower arrangement," thus enhancing the company's bottom line.

Know Your Legal Rights

Any person purchasing a funeral has the moral and legal right to purchase *only* what they want or really need, or think and/or know what the deceased would have preferred. Should there be a pre-need policy in effect for a specific amount, there is no legal requirement the survivor must spend the full sum of money on the funeral, which elevates only the bank account of the funeral home. The difference not spent may be better utilized toward the survivors living expenses that might have been the intention of the deceased all along. This last example is just another reason for pre-planning the inevitable.

The Funeral Industry is Highly Regulated

Regardless of what type of funeral a person chooses, it's very important to know the funeral business is regulated by federal, as well as state laws. The funeral director/salesperson knows how to dance and weave around these laws without actually breaking them, by pressing the emotional buttons of the person(s) making the arrangements that can greatly increase the cost of a funeral. This is Sales 101 - funeral style.

It's important to be aware of the regulations of the Federal Trade Commission. In addition, the laws of each state require every funeral director/salesperson to abide by strict consumer-oriented laws, stating your legal rights regarding different options and costs which must be on a required written price list. Being aware these federal laws exist can mean the difference of thousands of dollars saved in the pocket of the survivor(s). Researching before the inevitable happens is the key to money being spent wisely.

Use Your Ben Franklin Closing Page

Chapter Fifteen

Doublespeak: A Title by Any Other Name

George Orwell is Alive and Well
This extraordinary book written by Eric Arthur Blair, who gave himself the pen name George Orwell, was a prolific British writer. His most famous work, the novel *1984* is about a dictatorial society controlled and ruled by the Party. One of the major components used as a weapon against the masses, is *doublespeak:* The reversal of words and their true meaning. The more ambiguous the word or phrase, the more powerful it became. War meant peace, and ignorance meant strength.

Professional salespeople have been taught and have mastered the art of *doublespeak,* giving them the power to manipulate your thoughts to convince you the product, service, and terms being offered are exactly what you are looking for. *Doublespeak* is also used for the purpose of massaging the title of *salesperson* into a benign phrase that does not have the negative connotations the sales profession has earned with the public-at-large. *Doublespeak* can also be attributed to phrases used to maneuver you into signing a contract when you may not be ready, to make a decision, or you do not fully understand all the terms and conditions. Another variation of *doublespeak* is *spin*. Read chapter sixteen for examples of *doublespeak phrases* relating to the signing of a contract.

Avoiding the "S" Word

The most common method used to shy people away from "thinking or feeling" they are being *sold,* is to not speak or use any derivative of the word *"sales"*. It's one of the "dirty little secrets" within the profession. Salespeople prefer to address their title to a customer/client with *doublespeak*. People like to buy things, but they do not like to be *sold*. It just feels more comfortable to be *advised*. Companies have cleverly adapted alternative titles that are meant to make you, the consumer, feel psychologically at ease when speaking with any salesperson.

The charade continues in many forms. For example: Many companies, regardless of product or service, refer to their sales force as *producers*. However, it is highly unlikely you will ever see *producers* on a business card, even though that is exactly how the company views them. Salespeople either produce sales or they don't. If they don't produce sales, they're out of a job, because sales *must* produce profits for the company. If profits are not achieved everything else within the company is inconsequential.

Doublespeak Sales Titles - Minus the Word "Sales"

Regardless of the title, always be aware you are speaking with a salesperson, who is manipulating the conversation in order to make a sale. Closing the sale translates into a commission for the salesperson that is primarily based on the amount of money you spend. The following sales titles are a prime example of *doublespeak*.

Doublespeak Titles

Account Executive
Advertising Coordinator
Advertising Director
Advertising Manager
Advisor
Agent
Asset Protection Advisor
Automobile Representative
Business Broker
Business Development Associate
Business Intermediary
Business Sales Specialist
Call Center Representative
Certified Business Intermediary
Certified Financial Planner
Consultant
Coordinator
Customer Service Manager
Customer Service Representative
District Manager
Event Planner
Final Expense Specialist
Finance Manager
Financial Advisor
Financial Consultant
Fleet Manager
Franchise Specialist
Funeral Director
Investment Specialist
Leasing Consultant
Leasing Representative
Life Insurance Agent
Insurance Agent
Intermediary
Loan Manager

Loan Officer
Manufacturer Representative
Marketing Representative
Marketing Specialist
Mortgage Broker
Mortgage Originator
New Car Specialist
Pre-Need Counselor
Realtor
Real Estate Agent
Real Estate Broker
Recruiter
Route Service Specialist
Senior Account Executive
Senior Consultant
Service Advisor
Stock Broker
Stock Consultant
Travel Consultant
Wealth Management Specialist

Chapter Sixteen

More Doublespeak: When a Contract Isn't a Contract

Manipulative Terminology Used by Salespeople
The moment of truth has arrived. The salesperson thinks, or is at least hoping, a sale is within reach, and it may be time for the close. Be very aware and proceed with extreme caution, for you are signing a contract that can bind you into *financial oblivion*. Salespeople are taught *never* to call a contract by its rightful name any more than they would print *"salesperson"* on their business card. Consequently, don't expect to hear the word *sign* when it comes to what is known as *bottom line time* to *sign the contract*. The word has a tendency to generate *fear* and *mistrust* within the mind of many people.

Be certain you understand ALL the terms and conditions of the contract. If you do not, *don't sign*. Ask questions. If they are not properly answered, tell the salesperson you have to take the contract to your lawyer. After hearing those words, they will probably bend over backwards to explain every word. Should you still not be satisfied with any explanation given, it may be time to take a walk. It's important to remember if any part of the *sales performance,* up to and including, the signing of the contract does not pass your intellectual "smell test," your innate intuition has kicked in telling you not to proceed.

Devious doublespeak phrases have been created and used as closing techniques to "make you think" and "have you feel" the paper(s) you are about to sign are an informal exercise. Never forget. You are signing a legal contract. Period!

Doublespeak Closing Phrases

- Affix your name right here.
- Here is the agreement.
- I just need your assurance.
- If I could just get your autograph.
- If you could give me your John Henry, please.
- If you would just endorse your name for me.
- Just give me your John Hancock.
- Mark your signature right here. Please.
- Please acknowledge our agreement, right here.
- With your approval we can proceed.
- With your OK we can get the ball rolling.
- Your authorization is all that's required.
- With your endorsement, you will be a proud owner.
- With your endorsement we can proceed.
- With your signature we're good to go.
- Witness this and you'll be all set.

Chapter Seventeen

Open-Ended Questions

Listen to the Question Carefully
The purpose of an open-ended question is for you, the prospect, to provide the salesperson with information about your thoughts and feelings regarding the subject at hand. The hope is you will reply in the affirmative to any leading questions asked, thereby digging yourself into a hole deeper and deeper, basically talking yourself into a sale that may not be in your best-interest. The questions are generally broad in nature, in order to entice you into a positive conversation. Open-ended questions are a "tried and true" formula that has been an important part of any professional salespersons tool kit for many years.

Examples of Open-Ended Questions

- Can you give me an example of what you are looking for?
- Can you just see yourself being the proud of owner of . . .?
- Can you enlighten me regarding your problem?
- Who is the lucky person?
- What is it I can help you with?
- What benefit do you expect to derive from this information?
- What can I do to help?
- What do you envision as the next step?
- What else is it you wish to know about?
- What examples can you provide to me?
- What will it help you accomplish?
- Where would you like it delivered?
- When would you like it sent out?
- When would you like to take possession?
- Why would you want to wait?
- How does that make you feel?
- How may I help you?

Chapter Eighteen

Basic Human Emotions: Every Salesperson's Main Weapon

All Humans Have Emotions
As part of any comprehensive training session, every salesperson worth their salt is taught to look for (and push) the emotional buttons of the prospect they are speaking with. It's Sales 101.

Remain keenly aware. Use all your cognitive abilities and suppress the instinct of emotions when dealing with any salesperson, from the moment you meet up to the time you leave. This will serve you well throughout your life, regardless of what the service or product the salesperson is trying to sell you. Turn your emotions on after the sale.

Plutchik's Wheel of Emotions

Robert Plutchik
Professor Emeritus, Albert Einstein College of Medicine
October 21, 1927 - April 29, 2006

Professor Plutchik created his "Wheel of Emotions" in 1980 designating eight basic primitive emotions, and eight advanced. When dealing with any salesperson, use the following list he created, which identifies many universally important secondary feelings describing the human experience.

HUMAN EMOTIONS			RESULTS	
Emotion	**Opposite**	**Feeling**	**Feelings**	**Opposite**
Joy	*Sadness*	Optimism	Anticipation + Joy	*Disappointment*
Trust	*Disgust*	Love	Joy + Trust	*Remorse*
Fear	*Anger*	Submission	Trust + Fear	*Contempt*
Surprise	*Anticipation*	Awe	Fear + Surprise	*Aggression*
Sadness	*Joy*	Disappointment	Surprise + Sadness	*Optimism*
Disgust	*Trust*	Remorse	Sadness + Disgust	*Love*
Anger	*Fear*	Contempt	Disgust + Anger	*Submission*
Anticipation	*Surprise*	Aggression	Anger + Anticipation	*Awe*

Greed: The Ultimate Character Flaw

Of all factors related to the human psyche, greed is at the top of the list for any salesperson to exploit. It's one of the most impulsive emotional feelings specifically related to techniques they are taught to manipulate within the mind of all their prospects. Greed has been defined as "excessive or rapacious desire," especially for wealth or possessions. Greed is a noun that never stops.

In order to collect the highest commission possible, a salesperson can *sense* and *smell* when greed is pervasive within the person they are speaking with. Greed is one of the most important tools they take from their toolbox as much as they think necessary to "close the sale." Financial salespeople have taken the "greed button" to an art form. Countless people throughout history have lost multitudes of dollars, or purchased products and services that did not serve them well. Big ticket item salespeople play greed like a violin, piercing in on their client's ego, improper habits and any other base instincts they become aware of during the opening act of the *play* in progress. This process used by salespeople continues indefinitely. The information retrieved is then used as ammunition to push the "greed button" of their client/customer in order to close a sale. Mission accomplished!

There is nothing wrong with any person wanting the most, the biggest, or the best of anything, as long as the critical thinking process is never clouded. Caution is the key.

Chapter Nineteen

Splashy Headline Advertising: Internet - Print - Radio - TV

Grabbing Your Attention

The headline in any advertisement whether it is print or electronic media is equivalent to the barker at the amusement park trying to lure you into an attraction. All forms of sales have a common threaded purpose: Attract your attention to the offer, after which time, the salesperson will perform their "magical sales spell" thereby producing profits for the company and a commission for themselves. The game is the same, the only change is the technology.

Immediately after having been "emotionally overwhelmed" by the headline (which is the objective), all your protective antennas must become active, as the glaring headline is just the "frosting on the cake." The details of the purchase are in the disclaimers, as written about in chapter twenty. The following examples are tried and true headlines that scream at you on a daily basis.

Examples of Splashy Headlines

Act Now
All Reasonable Offers Accepted
All Contracts Accepted
Amazing Values
Anniversary Sale
Big Savings
Blow Out
Bonus Cash
Buy Factory Direct and Save
Buy One Get One Free
Call Now
Celebrate with Us
Clearance Sale
Construction Sale
Don't Wait - Call Now
End of Season Sale
Everything Must Go
Everything on Sale
Extraordinary Values
Fabulous Prices
Family Owned and Operated
Famous Brands at Discount Prices
Floor Sale
Free Admission
Free Appraisal
Free Analysis
Free Delivery
Free Drawing
Free Estimates
Free Exam
Free Information
Free Online Shipping
Free Seminar
Free Shipping
Free Quote

Get Today's Hot Deals
Great Reasons to Buy Now
Guaranteed Lowest Prices
Happy Birthday to Us – You Save
Having a Job Means Having a Ride
Holiday Specials
Hot Deals
Ladies Day Special
Lifetime Warranty
Lowest Financing Available
Lowest Prices Guaranteed
Make No Payments for Ninety Days
One Day Special
Order Now and Save
Price Includes Dealer Fee
Prices Discounted Below Cost
Prices Reduced
Rarely Discounted Brands
Reduce Your Electric Bill
Sales Event
Same Day Approval
Save High Energy Costs
The Call is Free
Three Days Only
We Will Not Be Undersold
We Will Meet or Beat Our Competitors
We Say Yes When Others Say No
While Supplies Last
Wholesale Prices to the Public
Your Credit Doesn't Matter
Zero Interest on All Approved Credit
Zero Interest – Today Only
Zero Interest with Approved Credit

Chapter Twenty

Asterisks and Disclaimers: Reading the Fine Print

The Devil is in the Details

The "devil is in the details" is a very important idiom to always keep in mind when dealing with the purchase of any service or product. There is, most assuredly, a negative price to be paid should you choose to ignore the details of any transaction.

Advertisements from any medium will present you with a bevy of disclaimers from headline attracting statements, such as those examples in chapter nineteen. Next time you see an ad on television, notice the disclaimer at the bottom of the screen. In most cases you cannot read it, for the print is too small and the time sequence is too short. The disclaimers are designed so you cannot possibly read the details. The advertisement is produced as an emotional inducement, nothing more-nothing less, designed strictly to entice you to have enough interest to contact the company by telephone, internet, or by physically driving to their place of business.

The same is true of radio advertising, as well, except with many of those disclaimers the announcer speaks so quickly it's impossible to intelligently understand what has just been said. That's the point. Just call or come down, and they will "take good care" of you. The problem is, the person(s) "taking care of you" is far more concerned about "taking care of themselves." Remain very cautious as the details of the transaction may not be advantageous to you. The difference between internet and print advertising as compared to radio and TV is, they allow the reader the opportunity to evaluate some of the true details of the service or product being offered, although a magnifying glass may be needed due to the very thought-out *reduced size* of the type and *remote location* on the screen.

Advertisements are built around a masterful form of creating the perception you are going to receive *something for nothing*, or a *terrific bargain*. The reality of the actual requirements and/or terms of your purchase may be quite different from the stated headline camouflaged within the small print that is preceded with an asterisk(s) that most assuredly refers to a disclaimer(s).

A One-Two Punch: Solicit and Sell

Step #1 - The ad enticed you to contact the company, by whatever means, be it direct mail, email or telephone, solicitation.

Step #2 - The job of the salesperson is to sway you from the ad that brought you to them, and *sell* or better yet, *up-sell* a service or product that will bring in the highest profit for the company. This, in turn spills over to the salesperson in the form of a higher commission.

The following examples are various disclaimers you may find after the asterisk(s), as the details become more complex. The only reason for the asterisk(s) and disclaimer(s) is for the legal protection of the company. If the companies really wanted you to hear or see the disclaimer(s) loud and clear, within any advertisement: The radio announcer would speak at a normal pace, the television ad would properly display the unreadable and quickly displayed fine print so it would be more legible, and the internet as well as print ads would not require a magnifying glass.

"Benefits 'Given' to the Consumer in the Headline, Can be 'Taken Away' by Disclaimer(s) in the Fine Print."

Examples of Disclaimers

Actual cost is based on specific hourly labor rate
Additional fees, charges and taxes may apply
Amenities not included
Annual membership fee is required
All items shown may not be in stock
All rights reserved
Available to first time buyers only
Based on room availability
Company not responsible for misprints
Contract required with purchase
Coupon advertisement must be mentioned when calling
Coupon duplicates are null and void
Coupon must be brought in at time of purchase
Customer loyalty program does not apply
Date of release is subject to change without further notice
Dealer fee not included
Dimensions are approximate. See associate for complete details
Exclusions may apply
Finance charge begins accruing from date of purchase
For more information speak with store representative
Free shipping excludes certain items
Ground floor delivery only
High beacon score required
High speed internet required

Individual results may vary
Installation charge applies
Interest deferred only for first ninety days after purchase
Limited color selection
Mileage estimates my vary
Minimum finance charge required monthly
Minimum purchase required
Most gems require professional care
Must use dealer financing
No rain checks allowed
Not valid with other coupons or discounts
Offer void during peak hours
Offer void where prohibited
Offers cannot be combined
On approved credit
One item per ad
Other limitations or restrictions may apply to some products
Penalty for early withdrawal
Person portrayed in ad are professional models
Photos are for illustration purposes only
Premium lots require additional fee
Prequalified contractors must be used
Price does not include options
Prices only good at the main store
Prices only good for one week
Prices subject to change
Prices vary depending on market conditions
Product has not been approved by the FDA
Product can only be purchased online
Promotional finance charge valid for first thirty days
Quantities are limited
Reorders subject to retail price
Restocking fee applied if returned
Sale offers are not available online
Screens are measured diagonally
Second item must be of equal value
See store for details

Select models only
Service agreement required with purchase
Shipping and handling fees extra
Software not included
Some merchandise not available in all stores
Some parts and labor is not included in contract
Some restrictions apply
Store reserves the right to limit quantities
Subject to change or cancellation
Subject to change without notice
Subject to credit approval
Subject to eligibility
Termination fee if cancelled
Upgraded amenities not included
Void where prohibited
W.A.C. (With Approved Credit)
Weight loss may be less than advertised
While supplies last
Zero percent is based on select models only

Chapter Twenty-One

Perception vs. Reality

Manipulative Language
It's important to be aware of the manipulative language salespeople have used for as long as anyone can remember. As time goes on, the list becomes longer due to changes in technology as well as the whims and values of society.

Logic First - Emotions Second
A manipulative picture within your mind will almost always induce your emotions not to utilize the Cost-Benefit-Value Analysis for the product or service being advertised in direct sales pitches. As previously mentioned, enjoy your emotions to the fullest after the sale is completed. You most probably know what is going to ring your emotional bell long before you read an ad or confront a salesperson.

Keep your emotions on the back burner during the *battle*. Making your purchase logically will enable you to enjoy it emotionally later.

The salespersons main weapon are the words they speak, day-in and day-out to their prospects, as they work to stimulate emotions in a positive light toward the service or product being offered. They're always honing their craft while subtly reeling the *fish* in, with whatever final *closing hook* they can conjure up that will snag *your* wallet catching them a commission.

You must always be aware of the preeminent tools in the salespersons *bag of tricks* they may choose to take out anytime they are speaking with you. Body language, expressive techniques and manipulative forms of *doublespeak* can penetrate into your reality the benefit(s) you *hope* you will receive after the sale. Remain very cautious anytime a salesperson appears too friendly. They are overdoing one of their techniques, and they may not even realize it.

The Five Human Senses

The five human senses of hearing, sight, smell, taste, and touch play a large part in the decision making process. Salespersons use these to their advantage, hoping to bypass your critical thinking process by inducing, then magnifying, the perception of an experience.

An example would be the car salesperson asking you to take a moment to sit in the driver's seat of the vehicle you are considering. By inviting you to sit in the showroom vehicle, this particular sales tactic is expected to bring forth instant gratification within your senses of touch and smell. A two-run homer for the salesperson. Playing with your natural senses or purposely talking to you ten or twenty feet from that brand spanking new car is designed to "set you up" by creating your own sensual panoramic views from the driver's seat.

A financial advisor/salesperson using the same tactics, can easily paint the picture for you to visually see yourself, sometime in the future, lying on the beach while the dividends are rolling in. The bakery owner/salesperson can place samples of their products on the counter, for you to sample using your senses of sight and smell, and the audiologist/salesperson can provide a test later *emphasizing* the discernible sounds you didn't hear well, in order to get you to purchase a hearing aid.

Everyone, regardless of title, be it the butcher, baker or candlestick maker is a salesperson. Therefore, it's important to maintain your rationality against your senses, when the decision to purchase or not, arrives. Take the time, to decide if your initial desire and perception of any product or service will meet and correctly conjoin on the same track as your critical thinking process.

Chapter Twenty-Two

Time-Tested Emotional Buzzwords and Phrases

Creating a Picture of Success
Be prepared to encounter the salesperson letting you know how top-notch and successful they are. The purpose is to imply, and draw a mental picture for you, of how successful and well-versed they are in their profession, thereby assuring you, they are looking out for your best-interest. This may or may not be true. Many buzzwords and phrases have been developed to place you at ease, thus assuring you that your worries are over and all your concerns will be properly addressed. Watch for plaques and awards hung in frames on the wall of the salespersons office. Some may spout million dollar sales awards, etc. They are propaganda developed to impress your senses, not your mind. As a potential client/customer, the accolades are of no consequence to you. Keep in mind, just because a salesperson is the recipient of a sales award, (if it's true) does not necessarily mean any previous client's best-interests were considered. Maybe they

were, maybe they were not. It's all about what the salesperson can do for *you* that matters.

Perception Accolades Used by Salespersons

- I'm the leading provider of widgets in the state
- I'm a member of the Million Dollar Round Table
- I'm the highest volume representative in the organization
- I'm an award winning advisor in the corporation
- I've been a top producer for many years
- I've sold more automobiles than anyone in the company

The statements listed above are of no value to *you,* as there is no way of knowing if there is truth to them, or they served the best-interest of the previous clients/customers. Even if the statement is correct, that does not necessarily mean the salesperson will be working in *your* best-interest. They are based on the "perception of assumption." To *assume* anything can be quite dangerous to your "financial health." Always keep within your thoughts any type of sales expressive technique(s) used for the purpose of disarming you. Never stop thinking: WIIFM. "What's In It for Me" You had better believe the salesperson is.

A List of
Emotional Buzzwords and Phrases

A Few Simple Steps
Absolutely
Act Now
Affordable
Amazing
American Dream
As Seen on TV
Attractive

Authentic
Bargain
Beautiful
Before There Gone
Biggest
Bonus Offer
Breakthrough
Buy One, Get One Free
Call Now
Cheap
Colossal
Confidential
Cram packed
Critically Acclaimed
Cutting Edge
Delicious
Direct to you
Discount
Easy to Use
Exit Strategy
Fabulous
Fantastic
Features
First Class
Free Delivery
Genuine
Gigantic
Globalization
Greatest
High Performance
High Tech
High Quality
Incomparable
Incredible
Just Received
King Sized
Leverage

Lovely
Lifetime Warranty
Limited Quantity
Limited Time Offer
Long Lasting
Low Cost
Luxury
Miracle
Miraculous
Money Back Guarantee
No Obligation
No Risk
Nothing Down
Nothing to Lose
Once in a Lifetime Offer
One Day Special
One of a Kind
Order Now and Save
Paradigm
Paradigm Shift
Passive Income
Personalized
Price Includes Dealer Fee
Prices Reduced
Prices Discounted Below Cost
Prices Slashed
Prime Time
Proven
Rare
Rarely Discounted Brands
Real McCoy
Reduce Your Electric Bill
Reduced
Remarkable
Revolutionary
Risk Free
Sales Event

Same Day Approval
Save High Energy Costs
Shocking
Solution
Spacious
Special Offer
Splendid
Stupendous
Sturdy
Sublime
Substantial
Succulent
Super
Superb
Superior
Super Charged
Super Duper
Ten-Fold
Ten Times Better
Terrific
Testimonial
The Call is Free
Three Days Only
Tremendous
Turnkey
Unbelievable
Unparalleled
Unprecedented
Unusual
Up-To-Date
Urgent
Value
Value-Added
We Will Meet or Beat Our Competitors
We Will Not Be Undersold
We Say Yes, When Others Say No
While Supplies Last

Wholesale Prices to the Public
Win-Win
Wisdom
Wonderful
Work Smarter, Not Harder
Your Credit Doesn't Matter
Zero Interest on All Remaining Stock
Zero Interest - Today Only
Zero Interest with Approved Credit

Chapter Twenty-Three

Sales Seminars: In-Person and On-Line

Selling Pie in the Sky
One of the most devious sales techniques playing on stage is the so-called *seminar,* whether it's in person or online. The sales tactics used for years are tried and tested programs that stimulate the emotions of greed and power, which are the twin bullets shot to pitch and sell everything ranging from financial seminars to business opportunities and get rich quick schemes that are hosted in hotel conference rooms, restaurants, and country clubs. Now they are being worked on the internet as *webinars,* some of which are the most creative in the history of sales. Regardless of title, the "so-called" main speaker(s) is a salesperson selling *hype* and *hope.* They might as well be donning a circus barker's hat, holding a candy-striped cane.

The opportunity to receive a free meal in a restaurant is one of the main attractions used for many years by promoters to lure an audience in like cattle to the slaughter for an *Information Seminar.* These so-called *seminars* have generally provided quality leads and hefty profit margins for their promoters behind the scenes, in addition to high commissions for the ringmaster-in-charge. Utilizing the power of the internet, the companies have kicked up the *seminar* to the *webinar* with less overhead, reaching a wider audience looking for the "pipe dream." This is a win-win situation for the company. Given the inexpensive economics and the ability to reach a mass audience, it is likely these *webinars* will be occurring in greater numbers than ever before. It's better to be overcautious than not cautious at all.

Perhaps, it may be possible to accomplish the goals presented by the salesperson at any of these so-called *seminars/webinars.* Then again: Perhaps not. However, should you decide to be physically present or view one, every red flag within your psyche must be on alert. Remember, the practiced script has been written and re-written to perfection many times over, leaving little opportunity for you to say *no* to the pitch, handing over your hard-earned money to the ringmaster. Proceed with *extreme* caution.

Chapter Twenty-Four

General Summation

Important Points to Remember

- Many salespeople have no conscience.
- If the sales pitch sounds too good to be true it most certainly is false.
- Never allow your emotions to overtake your logic.
- Never trust, or drop your guard during a sales pitch. Every claim must be substantiated.
- Meeting with a salesperson is all about retrieving your money. The more you give to the salesperson for any product or service, the less you will retain for yourself.
- Purchasing a product or service because you "want to believe it to be true" is a recipe for disaster.
- The more personal information the salesperson can learn about you, the greater their power increases to

- close the sale at your expense.
- If you are purchasing with your spouse, as an example, be cautious and buy as "one person." Never allow the salesperson to "play your emotions" against those of the other person. Price, color, size, etc. Should you need to discuss an issue in private, politely excuse yourselves, in order to coordinate a viable strategy, always working together as "one person." This tactic will serve you well.
- Whenever a salesperson is paid an incentive, in most cases being a commission, based as a percentage of the sale, always remember: You and your adversary have a different agenda when the subject of price, terms and conditions apply.
- Never, ever feel obligated or allow a salesperson to pressure you for a purchase.
- Create and analyze your Cost-Benefit-Value Analysis before you purchase.
- Should the negotiations with the salesperson fail, never hesitate or feel embarrassed to take a walk. Keep in mind: This strategy can be used as a successful tactic to achieve your goals.

Chapter Twenty-Five

Helpful Websites For Consumers

Automobile
AutoByTel.com
AutoCheck.com
AutoByTel.com
Cars.com
CarsDirect.com
CarChex.com (Extended Warranty Comparison)
Carfax.com
CarsYahoo.com
Edmunds.com (Automobile Information)
FuelEconomy.gov (Annual Fuel Costs)
Intellichoice.com (Costs and Trade-in Values)
KBB.com (Kelly Blue Book)
LeaseCompare.com (Automobile Leasing)
LeaseGuide.com (Automobile Leasing)

MyAutoloan.com
Nada.com (National Automobile Dealers Association)
NICB.org (National Insurance Crime Bureau - Lost or Stolen Vehicles)
TrueCar.com
VehicleHistory.gov (National Motor Vehicle Title Information System)

Consumer
AngiesList.com
BBB.org (Better Business Bureau)
SquareTrade.com (Independent Warranty Provider/Appliances and Electronics)

Financial
Aarp.org
Aadmm.com (American Association of Certified Daily Money Managers)
BankRate.com (Financial)
BretWhissel.net (Financial)
Diffen.com (Financial))
Dinkytown.net (Financial)
EFunda.com (Financial)
FinancialCalculator.org
Finra.org (Financial/Background check of investment persons)
Interest.com (Financial)
MoneyChimp.com
Mortgage-Auto-Loan-Calculator.com
MortgageCalc.com
Mortgage-Calc.com
ReverseMortgage.org (Reverse Mortgage Information)
ReverseMortgageGuides.org (Reverse Mortgage Information)
SaveAndInvest.org (Finra Broker Check)

Funerals
CelebrantInstitute.org (Funeral Information)
Funeralwise.com (Questionnaire for funeral plans)
Funerals.org (Funeral Consumers Alliance)
HomeFuneralAlliance.org (Funeral Information)
ThePartyOfYourLife.com (self-planning your own funeral)

Government
Consumer.FTC.gov (A bevy of consumer information)
FTC.gov (Federal Trade Commission)
HUD.gov (Housing and Urban Development)
Pueblo.gsa.gov (Government Publications)
SEC.gov (Securities and Exchange Commission)
USA.gov (Government Agency Websites)

Legal
Abanet.org (American Bar Association)
Nolo.com (Legal Information Provider)

Real Estate
Homes.com
HouseValue.com
HUD.gov (Housing and Urban Development)
RealEstateABC.com
RealtyTrac.com
Zillow.com

Suitability Forms (Annuities/Insurance)
FCSLA.org
NSSLIFE.org

Chapter Twenty-Six

Hollywood Films: Where Fiction and Non-Fiction Intermingle

Perhaps you have had the opportunity, or would like to take some time well-spent, to view the following list of films. They present a varied, entertaining, and real-world look into the lives of public and private financial market manipulators, corporate raiders, salespeople, and con artists.

Some movies portray stories relating specifically to the financial industry, others provide an insight into varied aspects of the average person's life, from economics to religion. Regardless of the basic plot and subject matter, the common thread is ego, power and greed, which generally translates to money. Some movies are fiction other films are non-fiction. A few are based on actual persons lives and/or events.

Unfortunately, opportunistic and unscrupulous governmental and financial market manipulators, corporate raiders, salespeople, and outright con artists, operate *specifically* with the sole thought of bringing in the "bottom line" by "closing the sale" or "the deal," regardless of the financial and/or human consequences strewn on the tracks, they leave behind.

The people portrayed in many of these films also procure a similar agenda, which is to ignite people's low level human instincts that are negative to their own self-interest. The objective in many cases is to provide some form of gain (generally being money) while camouflaging their strategies and techniques so the "marks" never become aware of the *con* that just took place.

A Fish Called Wanda
Arbitrage
Birthday Girl
Boiler Room
Casino Jack

Catch Me If You Can
Confidence
Corporate Raiders
Dirty Rotten Scoundrels
Elmer Gantry

Freakonomics (A Documentary)
Glengarry Glen Ross
Heartbreakers
Heist
House of Games
Inside Job (A Documentary)
Jerry McGuire
Leap of Faith
Matchstick Men
Maverick
Ocean's Eleven

Opportunity Knocks
Other People's Money
Paper Moon
Rounders
Salesman
   (A Documentary)
Six Degrees of Separation
The Big Kahuna
The Brothers Bloom
The Flim Flam Man
The Goods: Live Hard, Sell Hard
The Grifters
The Hustler
The Music Man
The Spanish Prisoner
The Sting
The Third Man
Tin Men
Two for the Money
Used Cars
Wall Street
Wedding Crashers

Chapter Twenty-Seven

A Final Thought: Benefits or Consequences

Every purchase you make will derive either a benefit or consequence. Obviously, you always want the benefit you deserve, having spent your money on purchasing the service or product that fulfills your needs and self-interest.

The natural laws of "Cause and Effect" and the "Law of Unintended Consequences," are especially relevant when dealing with any salesperson trying to sell you anything. Consistently maintain a conscious mindset using your critical thinking skills, while never letting your guard down. These are all necessary requirements as you dodge and weave the *bullets* many salespeople will *shoot at you* in order to make a sale, even if it's at your expense. It's reality 101. This book has been written with the philosophy of consciously maintaining that reality in order to achieve your objective(s). Refusing and/or choosing to ignore that reality will inevitably bring forth the consequences of your actions. Recognizing reality while maintaining self-interest can reap bountiful benefits in many ways.

Self-Interest: Best-Interest

These terms are expressed consistently throughout this book. When dealing with ANY salesperson, your foremost thought must be your own self-interest, which in many instances includes people important to you. The salesperson is also thinking of their self-interest as well. In many cases (unfortunately) it's all about receiving the highest commission possible, perhaps at your expense. Your goal is to purchase all products and services at a fair market price, the highest benefits and best terms possible. A natural "war" has been setup between both parties. The person who comes out on top is generally the best *negotiator.*

Never Forget: Amortize Every Important Purchase

Before any sale can be consummated, it must be amortized. Don't just amortize the reduction of principal and interest without thinking about lifestyle considerations such as your age, stability of occupation, how long you intend to hold the loan, etc. The list is endless.

Interest Rate versus Annual Percentage Rate

Every purchase of any substantial means must be calculated knowing the true APR. When figuring: Always keep in mind any *add-ons* or *up-charges,* as they must be calculated into the equation. The APR is the true and only reliable calculation, because it takes into account all fees and miscellaneous charges.

Cost-Benefit-Value Analysis

Analyze every aspect of your purchase to estimate, calculate and compare the benefits from the costs. Compare and contrast lifestyle consideration as well.

Appendix A

BEN FRANKLIN CLOSE - CRITICAL QUESTIONS
PLACE A CHECK IN THE <u>YES</u> OR <u>NO</u> COLUMN.
THE APPROPRIATE NUMBER OF CHECKS WILL HELP TO
DETERMINE AN ANSWER IN YOUR SELF-INTEREST.

Write the questions that are pertinent to the specific product or service you are looking to purchase. Quietly and calmly review the number of checks on each side in order to make rational decision.

QUESTIONS	YES	NO

Appendix B

BEN FRANKLIN CLOSE - PRE-PRINTED QUESTIONS
AFTER REVIEW, PLACE A CHECK IN THE
YES OR **NO** COLUMN.
THE APPROPRIATE NUMBER OF CHECKS WILL HELP TO
DETERMINE AN ANSWER IN YOUR SELF-INTEREST.

Some of the following questions are general in nature, while other pertain to various categories. Pick and choose the questions pertinent to your particular situation. Quietly and calmly review the number of checks on each side in order to make a rational decision.

QUESTIONS	YES	NO
Does the business require any learned technical skill? (**new/operating business**)		
Is the labor market difficult to fill? (**new/operating business**)		
Will the present owner stay on for a reasonable period of time? (**operating business**)		
Are the last 3-year IRS returns available? (**operating business**)		
Is the product/service in demand? (**new/operating business**)		
How profitable is the company? (**operating business**)		
Is the cash flow positive? (**operating business**)		
What is the ROE (Return on Investment)? (**operating business**)		
Do I really need life insurance? (think dependents, etc.) (**life insurance**)		
How much do I really need? (think dependents lifestyle, etc.) (**life insurance**)		
Which type is best for me? (Term, Whole Life, etc.) (**life insurance**)		
Which insurance is the most affordable for me? (compare companies) (**life insurance**)		

QUESTIONS	YES	NO
Should I replace my existing life insurance policy? **(life insurance)**		
Is the insurance company stable? (compare companies) **(life insurance/annuities)**		
Fixed? Variable? Equity Indexed? - (research, research, research) **(annuities)**		
Do I want to tie up my money for a long or short period of time? **(annuities)**		
Is the guaranteed income stream in the future, when I am older, important to me?		
I have to think about surrender charges, if necessary. **(annuities)**		
What are the policy expenses? (investment/ mortality fees, etc.) **(annuities)**		
Are there discounts available? (alarm systems, etc.) **(homeowners insurance)**		
Exactly what is covered? (building, contents, jewelry) **(homeowners insurance)**		
Exactly what is excluded from the policy? (flood, etc.) **(homeowners insurance)**		
Can I purchase options through a rider? **(homeowners insurance)**		
Is mold covered? (water damage, high humidity locations) **(homeowners insurance)**		

QUESTIONS	YES	NO
What does my policy cover? (drugs/cost/ doctor's visits/ cost) (**health insurance**)		
Is there a pre-existing clause? (**health insurance**)		
Does the policy allow me to go to the doctor of my choice? (**health insurance**)		
If not, what is the cost? (**health insurance**)		
Does my current doctor participate in your plan? (**health insurance**)		
Are there options regarding the deductible, versus the cost? (**health insurance**)		

www.ingramcontent.com/pod-product-compliance
Lightning Source LLC
Chambersburg PA
CBHW061509180526
45171CB00001B/97